MATALOONA
PUKHTUN PROVERBS

and

MIZH
A FRONTIER CLASSIC

OXFORD IN ASIA | Historical Reprints

MATALOONA

PUKHTUN PROVERBS

and

MIZH

A FRONTIER CLASSIC

Compiled and Edited by
Akbar S. Ahmed

OXFORD
UNIVERSITY PRESS

OXFORD
UNIVERSITY PRESS

Oxford University Press is a department of the University of Oxford.
It furthers the University's objective of excellence in research, scholarship,
and education by publishing worldwide. Oxford is a registered trade mark of
Oxford University Press in the UK and in certain other countries

Published in Pakistan by
Oxford University Press
No. 38, Sector 15, Korangi Industrial Area,
PO Box 8214, Karachi-74900, Pakistan

ISBN 978-0-19-070331-8

Typeset in Adobe Garamond Pro
Printed on 55gsm Book Paper

Printed by Kagzi Packages, Karachi

Contents

Foreword

To know a people, listen to their proverbs and poetry. At difficult moments in the jirgas that I conducted as Political Agent in the Tribal Areas of Pakistan, I noticed that a judiciously chosen Pukhto proverb could alter the mood of the gathering. The use of one of my favourite proverbs invariably elicited smiles and nodding of heads, while simultaneously working to rescue me from a difficult discussion. In one case in Waziristan, in the midst of a tense negotiation with a jirga, I was explaining my own delicate position caught between the demands of the tribe and the insistent instructions of far-away government which I represented. My predicament, I said, was captured by the proverb, 'on this side the staff, on that side the panther'. The English words lose their native pungency in the translation as the word for staff is *dang* and for panther it is *prang* which gives the proverb an onomatopoeic quality. The English equivalent is, 'between the devil and the deep blue sea'. The proverbs reflect the peripeteia, paradox, and predicament that mark our lives.

This compilation comprises of two small books first published by Oxford University Press in the 1970s—*Mataloona: Pukhto Proverbs* and *Mizh*, a monograph on the Mahsud tribe by Sir Evelyn Howell. Together they give us insights into the wit, honesty, humour, and wisdom of the Pukhtun (or Pukhtoon) peoples. Male and female, old and young, rich and poor, all take great pride in the richness of their shared heritage reflected in this volume.

Sir Olaf Caroe, who served with distinction in the North-West Frontier Province and at one stage was Governor, recounts in his Preface to *Mataloona* the time he was faced by a tense jirga which 'turned from scowls to a smile' when he quoted the proverb, 'patience is bitter, but its fruit is sweet'. In preparing *Mataloona*, I spent many an evening looking for the most exact translation of each Pukhto proverb or finding the nearest equivalent from other cultures; there are Arabic, Russian, Chinese, and Spanish proverbs and there is even Shakespeare. The diversity of sources establishes the scope, span, and sophistication of the Pukhto proverbs.

When discussing *Mataloona* it is well to keep in mind that this is the cultural treasure of the Pukhtun peoples who are considered the largest tribal society in the world today. Although they are found in the largest number in Pakistan, in the old Frontier Province, now called Khyber Pakhtunkhwa or KP, they are not restricted to that region. In fact, Pakistan's biggest city, Karachi, is considered the greatest Pukhtun city because of the large numbers of the community living in it. The Mahsud tribe, for example, dominates the transport system of the city. The other great concentration of Pukhtuns resides in the southern and eastern regions of Afghanistan. Pukhtuns also live in large numbers in India and in Western countries like the US and the UK.

Let me make a quick digression to introduce the Pukhtun peoples: Reflected in the two books that comprise this compilation is the core concept of Pukhtunwali (or Pukhtoonwali) or the code of the Pukhtun. The code is a way of life formed by ideas of hospitality, courage, respect for culture and language, and the practice of revenge. It is especially the last that often creates major problems for the Pukhtun in the modern world as some of the actions of the militant Pukhtun are driven by the code of revenge and clash with the norms and laws of the modern state. Indeed, I have found that in our contemporary twenty-first century world, Pukhtun proverbs often sum up well what is happening in Muslim tribal societies; for example: 'The Pukhtun who took revenge after a hundred years said, "I took it quickly."'

The Pukhtun have made a remarkable cultural and political contribution to the world. They have been kings in Afghanistan, presidents in Pakistan and India like Ayub Khan and Zakir Husain Khan respectively, the top movie stars of Bollywood, like Yusuf Khan known as Dilip Kumar, Mumtaz Jehan Begum or Madhubala, and Shah Rukh Khan to name just three, and led the Pakistan cricket team to World Cup victory—in the example of Imran Khan who is, as this foreword is being written, the Prime Minister of Pakistan. They have produced Badshah Khan, Abdul Ghaffar Khan, who proved that a warrior race can also promote and practice non-violence and peace, and was widely known as the 'Frontier Gandhi'. His son Abdul Ghani Khan was a true Renaissance man—poet, scholar, painter, and activist. Malala, the youngest winner of the Nobel Prize and her father, Ziauddin Yousafzai, are world renowned champions of education. We must not forget the Khan family and its world conquering squash players. Pukhtuns have been outstanding rulers of different states in the Indian subcontinent such as the Wali of Swat in Pakistan and the rulers of Rampur and Bhopal in India. History has recorded the extraordinary impact of rulers like Sher Shah Suri, who not only defeated and replaced the Mughal dynasty but in his brief tenure introduced some far-reaching and fundamental administrative reforms in India.

I had met Howell, author of *Mizh*, in the mid-1960s when I was at Selwyn College in Cambridge. One day, I found a handwritten note in my letter box. It was an invitation for tea from Howell. He wished to discuss the poetry of the great warrior-poet Khushal Khan Khattak that he was translating into English with his friend Caroe. He lived in a flat just across the college and I discovered that he had been the Political Agent of South Waziristan Agency. Little could I imagine that just over a decade later I would be stepping into his shoes as Political Agent of South Waziristan Agency and retrieving his *Mizh*.

I had read about *Mizh*, originally published in the 1920s, in Caroe's classic *The Pathans*, but I first encountered it in its entirety when in 1978 I came across a moth-eaten copy of the original book. I found it covered in dust and cobwebs in an obscure cupboard in the Political Agent's house in Tank. As Political Agent of South Waziristan Agency, I especially appreciated the frank discussion on the Mahsud tribe by Howell who had been first introduced to the Agency in 1905 and then, following the sudden murder of the Political Agent, was elevated to acting Political Agent of the Agency. That dramatic introduction to the Agency left a mark on Howell and created an affectionate fascination with the Pukhtun people and their land.

For all his enchantment, Howell did not underestimate the task of administering the Tribal Areas: 'A trans-border agency is a charge which imposes upon the holder a heavy strain, physical, mental, and, we may perhaps add, moral. It is not every officer, even amongst members of a picked corps, who is fit or by temperament apt to carry the burden, and even amongst the few who are there are fewer still who can stand the strain for long at a time.'

The Pukhtun targets individuals as symbols of something bigger that the victim represents, such as the state itself. That is why the Pukhtun shows little deference to or fear of attacking senior officials. In 1872, an Afridi seeking revenge for what he perceived as an attack on his honour by the British, killed the Viceroy of India, Lord Mayo, one of several in high office who lost their lives in such attacks over the years. Primary targets after the creation of the Tribal Areas in the late nineteenth century included the Political Agent, who was the head of the civil administration and the commandant of the paramilitary forces. In 1937, the Mahsud killed nine British military officers in an ambush in the Shahur Tangi pass when they did the impossible, that is wipe out an entire British brigade. In 1946, the Mahsud elder Mehr Dil of the Manzai clan, lunged at Jawaharlal Nehru in Razmak, thereby rallying other tribesmen for the creation of Pakistan. Nehru, who would become Prime Minister of India the next year, had come to the Tribal Areas to canvas support for his party but went back a disappointed man.

Howell wrote *Mizh* as an official confidential monograph for the Viceroy's office in Delhi. But his respect for the Mahsud cannot be concealed. There is a fascinating discussion in which Howell sums up the conversations he had with Mahsud elders in a single dialogue in which they discussed the merits of their respective civilisations.

Across the world, administrators in the newly formed United States of America were already dealing with tribal societies. In a mirror image of Howell and his Mahsud, Benjamin Franklin summed up the difference between the two systems by quoting a Native American elder who had been offered the opportunity to have members of his tribe educated at a local college by the government of Virginia. After thanking the government 'heartily,' the elder explained that he must decline:

Our Ideas of this Kind of Education happen not to be the same with yours.... Several of our Young People were formerly brought up at the Colleges of the Northern Provinces; they were instructed in all your Sciences; but when they came back to us, they were bad Runners, ignorant of every means of living in the Woods, unable to bear either Cold or Hunger, knew neither how to build a Cabin, take a Deer, or kill an Enemy, spoke our Language imperfectly; were therefore neither fit for Hunters, Warriors, or Counsellors; they were totally good for nothing. We are however not the less obliged by your kind Offer, tho' we decline accepting it; and to show our grateful Sense of it, if the Gentlemen of Virginia will send us a dozen of their Sons, we will take great Care of their Education, instruct them in all we know, and make *Men* of them.[1]

Franklin's respect for tribal traditions and the tribesman's insistence on letting his people be 'men' like their forefathers anticipates Howell in Waziristan. The difficulties in administering the Mahsud and the egalitarianism inherent in Mahsud society come through in a quote Howell recounts from a Mahsud elder: either 'blow us all up with cannon, or make all eighteen thousand of us Nawabs [chiefs]'. When Howell speaks of the Political Agents as 'custodians of civilisation dealing with barbarians,' he sums up the response of the Mahsud elders:

> A civilisation has no other end than to produce a fine type of man. Judged by this standard the social system in which the Mahsud has been evolved must be allowed immeasurably to surpass all others. Therefore let us keep our independence and have none of your 'qanun' [law] and your other institutions which have wrought such havoc in British India, but stick to our own 'riwaj' [custom] and be men like our fathers before us.

'After prolonged and intimate dealings with the Mahsuds,' concludes Howell, 'I am not at all sure that, with reservations, I do not subscribe to their plea.' After due consideration, Howell admits to agreeing with the Mahsud elder. It is a stunning admission of imperial failure, but also reflects the integrity and humility of Howell. Colonial intervention in the Tribal Areas was perhaps best summed up by a senior British officer upon reading Howell's *Mizh*: 'What a record of futility it all is!'

The affection for the Pukhtun that Howell and Caroe exhibit is genuine. I was privileged to meet both towards the end of their lives. They spoke warmly and constantly of the Pukhtun people and their lands. Looking back on his time in Waziristan from the tranquillity of Cambridge in England, Howell had shared his sentiments shortly before he died with his friend Caroe, who wrote to me:

---

1. Edmund S. Morgan, ed., *Not Your Usual Founding Father: Selected Readings from Benjamin Franklin*, (Yale University Press, 2006), 53.

When I met him in Cambridge about four years ago he said so many years had gone by. But he would feel happier in the mountain ranges of Waziristan. It was, he said, precisely because that was the most dangerous period of his life that it had become the period that he loved most. Often in his dreams he found himself in Waziristan, and his heart flying in those precipitous gorges.

Examples of Caroe's love of the land and the people of the Frontier are numerous. In his Preface to *Mataloona* he cites my own Introduction in which I quote him approvingly '... as he drove through the Margalla pass just north of Rawalpindi and went on to cross the great bridge at Attock, there was a lifting of the heart and the knowledge that...he had come home.' When I was completing my PhD in London in the 1970s, Caroe invited me with my wife Zeenat, and our two small children, Amineh and Babar, to his home in Steyning in the south of England. He had written with great admiration of Zeenat's grandfather, the Wali of Swat. At home, he pointed out the year the house was constructed, 1707. The same year, he said, the Emperor Aurangzeb died and the downfall of the Mughal dynasty began. He picked us up at the railway station and after a leisurely lunch dropped us back. I recall he drove at terrifying speed along the narrow, winding, country side roads of West Sussex.

When I was appointed Political Agent of Orakzai Agency in the mid-1970s, Caroe wrote me a letter in which he asked me, when next I visited the Samana rest house on the ridge which reaches almost 8,000 feet, I should look towards the west. He had planted several trees there when he was posted in the province three decades ago. The Samana Ridge is of course famous in history for the fierce battles that took place there between the British and the tribes. After unpacking at Samana on my first visit, I went out to have a look. Sure enough standing in silhouette overlooking the spectacular vista were Caroe's trees now grown to their magnificent size. Caroe was thrilled at the news.

In the epilogue to his celebrated book, *The Pathans*, Caroe called me a 'friend', provided the excellent aforementioned Preface to *Mataloona*, and in a handwritten letter dated 12 July 1979, sent not long before his death, wrote: 'I would like to tell you of my appreciation of what you have done, and are doing.' Back in 1947, Caroe's love of the Pukhtun may have cost him his job as Governor of the Frontier Province. The

Indian Congress accused him of being too close to the Muslim League
and manoeuvred to have him replaced.

Although *Mizh* was written in the 1920s it remained a confidential
government document. The result was that the foremost scholars of
Pukhtun tribes did not have access to it. For example, Fredrik Barth in
his influential *Political Leadership Among Swat Pathans* (1959) does not
mention the book. Even after OUP finally published *Mizh* in 1979 it
remained little-known outside a limited readership. It was not helped
by one or two curious and hostile reviews. Although Olaf Caroe, the
authority on the Pathans, had called it the 'most penetrating of all tribal
studies,' Dr M. E. Yapp in the *Bulletin of the School of Oriental and
African Studies* dismissed it in a sniffy and mean-spirited review as, 'rather
a disappointing account that scarcely deserves the praise lavished on
it by Caroe and by Dr Akbar Ahmed…for it lacks any real analysis of
the Mahsuds.' Yapp is irate that *Mizh* does not discuss subjects like the
economy and so forth, blaming Howell for something he did not promise
the reader. If Yapp had looked at the subtitle he would have noted that
the book is called, 'a monograph on government's relations with the
Mahsud tribe'.

There are lessons for us: of course both authors, Howell and Caroe,
represent the interests of the British Empire which was a straightforward
colonial enterprise. But we learn lessons from them in administration;
and both held important posts: Howell worked as Resident, Waziristan,
and Caroe was Governor of the Frontier Province. Those were difficult
posts in turbulent times. Yet in spite of onerous official duties these
officers sought to learn about the language and culture of the people
they administered. The very fact that they produced a translation of one
of the great poets of the Pukhtun people after they had retired and were
back in England is an illustration of their affection and respect. Alas
this contrasts with the indifference of post-Independence local officers,
with some honourable exceptions, to their charge. Very few books have
been produced about culture, traditions, and history of the people these
Pakistani officers administered.

The old Frontier Province, now KP province, which is the core
territory of the Pukhtun peoples, has seen dramatic change over the
last century. In the late nineteenth century the British created the tribal

agencies to act as an administrative buffer zone between Afghanistan and British India. Lord Curzon, the Viceroy of India, who in a moment of despair believed that there would be no peace in Waziristan until 'the military steam-roller had passed over the country from end to end' to quell the tribes, had great faith in the newly formed tribal agencies and in particular the Political Agents who ran them.

In 1947, the Frontier Province became part of Pakistan and the tribal agencies along the border were renamed the Federally Administered Tribal Areas, each headed by a Political Agent. The brutal Frontier Crimes Regulation from the British colonial era was kept in place and only removed after the tribal agencies were merged with the KP province in 2018. In the meantime, after 9/11, this area became a military theatre for the war on terror as American, Pakistani, and Afghan troops engaged with tribal entities in the midst of shifting alliances and confused objectives in pursuit of Al Qaeda and Osama bin Laden. Bin Laden was discovered and killed hiding in Abbottabad, a part of the KP province. Waziristan became perhaps the most attacked region in the world for the newly commissioned drone as a weapon of destruction. In the process not only were hundreds of thousands of people in the tribal areas dislocated, many having to flee from their homes, but the disruption of economic and political life still continues to impact their lives. In the late summer of 2019 the districts of the former FATA held their first ever elections for the KP assemblies. Sixteen general seats were contested with a further five reserved for women and minorities. Women participated and also stood for elections. Considering the area and its history the process passed peacefully enough although firing was reported in the Mohmand district, which was once Mohmand Agency. The elections were the final act in the absorption of what once were the Tribal Areas into the main political body of Pakistan.

Although over the span of the last hundred years when so many aspects of Pukhtun culture have been shaken and even destroyed—religious and traditional leadership has been especially affected—we can still recognise and appreciate *Mataloona* which defines and discusses Pukhtun culture. In *Mizh* we recognise the wisdom and pride of a tribal people.

There remains the danger of romanticising the Pukhtun in their hills; to see them through Orientalist eyes as the 'noble savage'. In fact, Caroe once told me he and I were both guilty to some extent of promoting a romantic image of the Pukhtun which may not have been entirely correct. My own experience however in meeting tribal peoples, thousands of men and women, old and young, across the land, is of a people that are wise, generous, hospitable, brave, and dignified. What has always struck me is the dignity of the Pukhtun. They are aware of their predicament in the modern world yet carry themselves with honour.

While we cannot condone violence especially of the kind we have seen in Pakistan after 9/11, the militant attacks on women, children, hospitals, and schools, Pakistan urgently needs to understand Pukhtun society and culture. In a profound way the social eruptions that have emerged from the Tribal Areas recently such as the Tehrik-e-Taliban (TTP) and the Pashtun Tahafuz Movement (PTM) are an expression of the rupture in Pukhtun society. It is not surprising either that these movements are led by young men from Waziristan. Because it speaks of Pukhtun rights and grievances, PTM has far wider support among Pukhtuns than the Pakistani leadership realises. The out-of-touch Pakistani leadership, especially the urban part of it, has little understanding and even less sympathy for the Pukhtun. It is they who are almost entirely to blame for the wars and problems of the Pukhtun.

Reading *Mataloona* and *Mizh* is a good first step to understand not only Waziristan, but also the Tribal Areas of Pakistan. While *Mataloona* shares the wisdom and insights of the Pukhtun for people of all ages and cultures, *Mizh* allows us to think of how to deal—or not to deal—with tribes in the modern world. Together, they should also dispel the idea that Pukhtun culture somehow lacks cultural sensitivity and sophistication. Those in Islamabad and Karachi who have little idea of Pukhtuns and think of them as backward and primitive would do well to read *Mataloona* and *Mizh*.

Neither Howell nor Caroe were scholars sitting in dark and dank offices surrounded by musty books and relying on obscure research to write about tribal people. They not only served in some of the most difficult posts in the Pukhtun lands, but wrote about them in the saddle, as it were. In contrast, the older generation of Pakistani officials has had little time for reading or writing apart from a few exceptions. The younger generation is preoccupied with existentialist issues of violence, terrorism, policy, and government changes that keep it unsettled. The result is that we do not benefit from their experiences in the field.

The tradition of the scholar-administrator has not entirely died out however, I am glad to report. Ghulam Qadir Khan Daur, a member of the local Daur tribe of Waziristan and senior civil servant of Pakistan, is an honourable exception. His book *Cheegha* is a powerful *cri de cœur* from and about Waziristan. There are other honourable examples as well. In a recent *Daily Times* article about Sahibzada Riaz Noor's book of poetry, *The Dragonfly and other Poems*, which had a foreword by Riaz's mentor Ejaz Rahim, I described the two distinguished Pakistani civil servants who had served in the Khyber Pakhtunkhwa province. Their poetry and their love of the Pukhtun people, their mutual camaraderie and public profile, I wrote, make them the Pakistani equivalent of Howell and Caroe.

I am personally grateful and delighted that OUP Pakistan is publishing *Mataloona* and *Mizh*. It has been an exhausting struggle to see the present volume in print as I was nervous in case the two books were lost to the reader. I would like to express my gratitude to two members of the OUP Pakistan in particular who made the republication possible and appreciated its significance—Raheela Baqai and Ghousia Ali. I am also grateful to Aamna Aziz for her editorial services. My special acknowledgement of Zeenat Ahmed who supported this project from its earliest days and has continued to oversee it to its present incarnation. Her enjoyment of *Mataloona* in particular is a delight to see and her enthusiasm has touched our children. I would like to dedicate this edition to her except that *Mataloona* is already dedicated to a great patron of Pukhtun culture and the Pukhto language, her grandfather, the former Wali of Swat.

Professor Akbar S. Ahmed,
Ibn Khaldun Chair of Islamic Studies
School of International Service
American University
Washington DC

26 June 2020

Book I

MATALOONA
PUKHTO PROVERBS

translated by

AKBAR S. AHMED

with a preface by

SIR OLAF CAROE

To Babaji
who has come to symbolise the best of
pukhtoonwali beyond the confines of his role as
the Wali of Swat.

Preface

Akbar S. Ahmed could not have paid such as me a greater compliment than to ask for a few introductory words to his fascinating collection of Pukhto proverbs. The memory is fresh of an occasion fifty years back, when I was learning the Pukhto language, and Qazi Rahimullah of Abdara, my teacher, told me that an ability to quote the apt *matal*-proverb is one way to the heart of the Pukhtoon. And so it proved once with an angry Mohmand *jirga* at Shabqadar, who turned from scowls to a smile when told that patience is bitter but its fruit is sweet:

صبر تریخ دے میوه ئ خوږه ده

In Persian and Urdu the word for a proverb is (مثل) *masal*, spelt with the letter *se*, but I am reliably told that Mr Ahmed is right in telling us that in Pukhto the word is pronounced *matal*, plural *mataloona*—probably harking back to the Arabic pronunciation of *se* as *th*, but God knows, *khudai khabar!* He himself in an eloquent Introduction, has given good reasons to convince the reader that proverbs are 'of the earth earthy', in each tongue a mirror of popular wisdom and of that peculiar humanity which is humour at the disposal of every people in its own way. I will not attempt to rival his analysis, for none could be better. Let me only say that the reading of these pithy sayings brings back the sights, the sounds, the very scents of village, field and mountain in that delectable land, making the longing to return almost unbearable. In the echo of the words here printed the old companionships are born again.

This is a second edition, in which it is good to see that the author has given fresh insight into the Pukhtoon feeling by adding in all cases a literal translation of the Pukhto words. For it does not suffice to tell readers who do not know Pukhto that

الوتے مارغه په لاس نه راځی

is equivalent to an injunction not to cry over spilt *milk*, when it is the *bird* which is flown and will not return. This is not to decry Mr Ahmed's skill in finding equivalents in English and other languages, a skill born of reading in many fields.

It is tempting joyfully to catch, and argue over, many of these *mataloona*, but I must refrain. There is heartbreak in some of the sayings, as in 'he who laughs much will weep also many tears' or 'in an old tree every calamity is wont to nest', or 'a woman's lot is either a home or the grave'. In many others there is the homely delight to be had from horse or cow, dog or donkey, cat or other pet of the house. Even the frog has his place. There is one interpretation I would question:

اے خوشحال ختکه - په درنو دروند په سپکو سپکه

O Khushal Khattak, heavy with the heavy, light with light.

Does this mean, as the author suggests, that the true gentleman suits himself to his company, is great with the great, humble with the poor? As in

چه پخپله ځان ته خان وائ خان نه دے

He who calls himself a Khan is no Khan.

That way of thought corresponds with another of Khushal's verses which I once translated:

> ...*Is lowly with the low, but strong to impress*
> *High looks upon the proud...*

Or does it mean, as an eminent Pukhtoon friend tells me, that to those of worth the poet's verses have value, while to the worthless they seem trifles? It is one of the delights of proverbs that they are so often open to various interpretations.

All praise to Akbar S. Ahmed for a moving compilation from the folklore of a lovable people. His work will call many who care for that land and people to cross once more the bridge at Attock before we pass on.

هر چاته خپل وطن کشمیر دے

To every man his own country is Kashmir. But there are many still, I am persuaded, not themselves of that land, who think of the Pukhtoonkhwa as their Kashmir—remembering the view of Lakasar from Peshawar on a spring morning, or the pine-clad shoulders of Ilam rising from the valley of Swat,

چرته چه زړه خی هلته ښپے خی

Where the heart goes, the feet follow,
or Home, sweet home!

Sir Olaf Caroe.
Steyning,
Sussex.

May 1974

Foreword*

The idea of collecting and translating Pukhto proverbs came up when Akbar was doing a course with us at the Academy earlier this year. This would be the first attempt of its kind. I readily accepted to give this project the cover of the Academy as I hoped it would encourage similar works on the various cultural regions of Pakistan.

It is amply illustrated from this collection that proverbs reflect a great deal of the social thinking of a people. To have an idea of how the rural people would think and react (as illustrated through their local proverbs) certainly helps in understanding their problems and finding solutions. In this way they offer an important clue to scholars and social scientists for further research. I am confident that this form of knowledge can be put to good use at our Academy. I hope that future participants at the Academy will be encouraged to contribute similar works which go a long way in giving us a complete and coherent picture of rural and traditional life in Pakistan.

Mr Akbar S. Ahmed, CSP, is to be complimented for putting together the Pukhto proverbs and working their translations so well (ably assisted, as he explains in his Introduction, by literary friends), and for being the pioneer in this type of publication and research work at the Academy.

Shoaib Sultan Khan, CSP
Director, Pakistan Academy for
Rural Development, Peshawar.

19 April 1973

---

*To the first edition published by the Pakistan Academy for Rural Development, Peshawar, May 1973.

9

Introduction

'Take fifty of our current proverbial sayings…they embody the concentrated experience of the race, and the man who orders his life according to their teaching cannot go far wrong', an English giant of literature has argued. As commonsense advice this is probably as true of the English as of almost any other society including the Pukhtoons (southern tribes, like Khattaks, soften their 'kh' to 'sh' and thus Pushtoon).

Proverbs are the concentrated wisdom of the ages; often the dark sayings of wise men. To know and study folklore, local priorities, or popular superstitions one can do no better than turn to proverbs. Proverbs can be considered from many angles: their philosophy, their origin, their style, and the importance of proverbs in folklore. However, due to their misty birth we must often leave their origin unexplained or choose between several explanations.

The two sources of proverbial wisdom appear to be:

1. The common man's proverbs derived from distilled experience, (e.g. A bird in the hand is worth two in the bush). These in Pukhto are live, visceral, and often earthy.
2. The wise man or oracle whose utterances were the result of reflection and were received as rules of life by the people. His comments eventually became familiar sayings, bywords, proverbs, or *mataloona* (singular *matal*). The sayings of these philosophers, authors, and poets became household homilies over time.

Both sources contribute largely to the mainstream of Pukhtoon culture as proverbs are commonly and popularly used in conversation at all social levels. Many Pukhto proverbs are in verse. A good example is the hortatory verse of Rahman Baba:

کوهے مه کنه د بل سری په لار کښے
چرے ستا به د کوهی په غاړه لار شی

Whoso diggeth a pit for another shall fall therein.

The great Pukhto poets like Rahman Baba, Abdul Hamid, and Khushal Khan Khattak have contributed immensely to the number of Pukhto proverbs. These have been left out; it is hoped that some enthusiast will put a collection of these under one cover in the future.

Pukhto proverbs rarely fail to attract the listener by their onomatopoeia and rhymes. Their actual strength lies, however, in the wisdom that they embody and their conscious underlining of Pukhto themes: the code of chivalry and honour imposed not only upon a segment of society but upon all those who would call themselves Pukhtoon. The Pukhtoon must then live up to the expectations envisaged in Pukhto concepts. Pukhtoon as a complimentary adjective is not restricted to those who simply speak the language.

This small anthology of Pukhto proverbs and their translations is a personal and subjective exercise. There will be cases of notable omissions: there will be those *mataloona* where the reader might prefer his own translation. He is welcome to it. No finality is advocated or claimed. As a rule those *mataloona* of a more general nature have been selected and those reflecting inter-tribal rivalries or strictly local prejudices have been omitted. The Pukhto proverbs have been placed in alphabetical order.

It is to be noted that sometimes not the exact but the nearest equivalent sense in translation whether in prose or verse has been used: sometimes the English version of proverbs from other countries has been given. It is a striking tribute to the essential oneness of man that similar emotions and ideas find an echo in such diverse areas and peoples. The translation is often free, conveying the sense rather than the literal. Sometimes however only the literal translation can preserve the power and the pungency of the original. All the proverbs have literal translations as well. Only where the English proverb is almost identical to the literal translation is the latter omitted. Where the literal translation appears awkward or esoteric on its own the equivalent corresponding proverb hopes to give it clarity, meaning, and dimension. The English equivalent is given first in Roman type and the literal translation follows in italics.

یو خوا ډانگ دے بل خوا پرانگ دے

Between the devil and the deep blue sea.
On this side the staff, on that side the panther.

In Pukhto *mataloona* is collected the wisdom and good sense garnered over a thousand years and from places that range from the peaks of the Hindu Kush to kingdoms along the Ganges.

They embody and illuminate the customs and spirit of Pukhtoon society which includes in its embrace the various Pukhto speaking tribes and sub-tribes that lie spread across Sir Mortimer Durand's line. Dating back beyond the confines of written history they often reflect in tone and sentiment some of the patriarchal wisdom of the ancient Palestinean peoples. Thus the *matal*, preceding the written word, comes down orally from generation to generation.

The proverbs have been forged on the anvil of wisdom by the hammer of time. Their robust force and marked jingling rhyme lends easily to their commitment to memory. The *mataloona* are now part of the atmosphere of the land; with a stroke they depict reality and life. In their pith they maintain a degree of studied nonchalance and a mature understanding of reality. The *matal* catches a mood or caps an argument, but always sums up a delicate moment of communication. It is the most concise, forceful, and rhythmic expression of the Pukhtoon language and temperament.

Pukhto proverbs form a rich lode for serious sociological study; they are like sociological nuggets embedded in the frontier hills and Pukhtoon culture. Sometimes plainly earthy, sometimes deeply esoteric, now pondered buckling on the breastplate before battle, and now sitting, in council in the *hujra*, they contain illustrative social attitudes and cultural patterns offering insight and clues to the norms and mores of Pukhtoon society. A study of these will open a window to Pukhtoon culture and the Pukhtoon mind. For they reflect the magic of the mountains, the joy and zest for life, the grim reality of poverty, the warmth of hospitality, and the priceless charm of wisdom.

This collection of *mataloona* hopes to give an impression of the elements that make up the concept of the ideal type in *Pukhtoonwali*: the elements of hospitality and modesty, honour and balance, and the presence of deep Islamic themes. The essence of the Pukhto language and the elements of the Pukhto concept are well illustrated by the *matal*.

Khushal Khan Khattak, in verse, thus honours the Yusufzai for upholding bravery in war and hospitality at home:

یوسف زئ میر افغان دی - هم د تورے هم د خوان دی
ننگ لری پښتانه واړه - ولے ننگ له د یو غواړه

'The nobles of the Afghans are Yusufzais,
Hard in battle-field and hospitable at home,
All Pukhtoons possess the sense of honour,
None, however, can vie with them.'

The other elements which make up the spirit and ethos of *Pukhtoonwali* also find expression in the popular *matal*. For instance,

Revenge (*badal*):

پښتون سل کاله پس بدل واغست وئیل ئے چه زر م واغست

The Pukhtoon who took revenge after a hundred years said, I took it quickly.

Honour (*nang*):

په سلو مِ مر کے په یو مِ پر مه کے

(*Oh God*) *kill me by a hundred* (*men*) *but let me not be shamed for one.*

Honour, that universal measure of chivalry in any age and society, is a recurring theme:

قول و بول په ژوندون نشی نوروله
ښکه خان په قول وژنی پښتانه

As long as he lives, he'll never change his promise.
To honour his word, the Pukhtoon will give his life.

The basic philosophy of life in Pukhtoon culture is the philosophy of dynamic movement, of action as an end. It is a strong, virile, bold philosophy:

دَ پروت ازمری نه گرځینده گیدړ ښه دے

An active jackal is better than an inactive lion.

Here is a man's world. And here is the traditional no-nonsense patriarchal society:

چرته ډب وی هلته ادب وی

Where there is discipline there is social order.

In an unabashedly male-oriented social fabric the role of the woman is strictly confined:

ښځے له یا کور دے یا گور دے

For the woman either the house or the grave.

Hovering over all these facets of life is a cloud of fatalism. Though this would appear in direct contrast to the bolder and braver calls to action, this is to be understood less as fatalistic (as we use the word) and more as a consciousness of those powerful and irresistible currents that flow about a man living in an environment where guns, violence, and sudden death are part of a way of life. A sun-baked gut-felt philosophic acceptance of reality on all levels of existence:

په منډه نه ده په تنده ده

*It is not the running around but that which is written on the forehead
(or in one's luck).*

چه لاړشے تر بلخه در سره ده خپله برخه

Even if you go to Balkh, you take your share of destiny with you.

The single most distinctive quality of the Pukhtoon is his individuality. This ensures a certain continuing strength of character and maturity. He is not easily swept away by fancy ideas. On the other hand, this very quality ensures that in his desire to remain untrammelled and unbound he will invariably remain disunited. It is remarkable that the word *tarboor* for cousin also commonly means rivalry or enmity.

Perhaps Khushal Khan best summed this up in his famous lament:

كه توفيق دَ اتفاق پښتانه مومى
زورِ خوشال به دوباره شى په دا خوان

'If they reject disunity, the Pukhtoon bane
Old Khushal will be born once again.'

I would like to reproduce the impressions of one of the earliest and most perceptive Englishmen to write about the Frontier peoples. Elphinstone arrived decades before the soldiers and statesmen who were to play out their roles in the Frontier drama. His observations, however, still remain perhaps the most objective, accurate, and comprehensive:

But an English traveller from India, would view them with a more favourable eye. He would be pleased with the cold climate, elevated by the wind and novel scenery, and delighted by meeting many of the productions of his native land. He would first be struck with the thinness of the fixed population, and then with the appearance of the people; not the fluttering in white muslins, while half their bodies are naked, but soberly and decently attired in dark-coloured woollen clothes, and wrapped up in brown mantles, or in large sheep-skin cloaks. He would admire their strong and active forms, their fair complexions and European features, their industry and enterprise, the hospitality, sobriety, and contempt of pleasure which appear in all their habits; and above all, the independence and energy of their character. In India, he would have left a country where every movement originates in the government or its agents, and where the people absolutely go for nothing; and he would find himself among a nation where the control of the government is scarcely felt, and where every man appears to pursue his own inclinations, undirected and unrestrained. Amidst the stormy independence of this mode of life, he would regret the ease and security in which the state of India, and even the indolence and timidity of its inhabitants, enable most parts of that country to repose. He would meet with many productions of art and nature that do not exist in India; but, in general he would find the arts of life less advanced, and many of the luxuries of Hindoostaun unknown. On the whole, his impression of his new acquaintances would be favourable.

The Pukhtoon way of life has been the most distinct of all the races of the subcontinent. It had to be. Their hunting grounds were uncharted turbulent ethnic oceans where the vast rivers of central, western, and southern Asia met; their boundaries were self-imposed and elastic: Baghdad to Delhi, Moscow to Canton. Their roles were varied: captains and kings, horse-trading and money-lending. And always the steep mountains to define, limit, shield, and form the very marrow of the Pukhtoon.

Here life and its contours take on other priorities. In the overwhelming poverty of the mountain life cultural tones are set. Pukhtoon greetings: *staray ma shay*—the dream-wish for total virility and physical energy— 'may you not get tired'—and the answer *khawar ma shay*—'may you never see poverty'—represent clear cut and recognised yearnings of the subconscious: health and affluence to keep at bay the twin spectres of palsied infirmity and poverty.

One purpose of this collection is to give a glimpse of the vast treasure of *mataloona* awaiting that reader who is prepared to collect for himself similar precious gems for his own treasure chest.

This collection is offered as a contribution to lovers of this culture and language. It is hoped that the English translations, though often rough and ready, will bring the pleasure and wisdom of the *matal* to a wider audience. I wish to confess that I am no scholar of the language but hope to have made up in enthusiasm and affection for what I lacked in knowledge. For me it has been a delightful and rewarding exercise.

Sir Olaf Caroe caught the mood, 'for the stranger who had eyes to see and ears to hear, always as he drove through the Margalla pass just north of Rawalpindi and went on to cross the great bridge at Attock, there was a lifting of the heart and a knowledge that, however hard the task beset with danger, here was a people who looked him in the face and made him feel he had come home.'

The deep knowledge and courtesy of the Pashto Academy and Pashto Department of the University of Peshawar have been availed of. Among other friends who have helped discuss, sift, and polish this collection, I wish to thank Syed Sarfaraz Ali and Mohammed Salim, my *ustaz*, who have spent many hours showing and teaching me *Pukhtoonwali* by personal example, and Miss Zebunnissa Alamzeb who provided indefatigable secretarial assistance. Qalander Mohmand was good enough to go through the final drafts with splendid insight. I also wish

to thank Mr Shoaib Sultan Khan, Director of the Rural Academy, who
has served these areas and people with great affection during his career
and who responded to the original idea of this booklet with typical and
complete support.

Finally, I would like to express my gratitude to Sir Olaf Caroe for
writing the Preface which I consider a singular honour for the book
and its major embellishment. Sir Olaf is one of the dying breed of giant
Frontiersmen cast in the classic mould: those writers-statesmen-soldiers
who created history across the Frontier canvas by day and wrote it in
lonely tents by night. He has immortalised both himself and his subject
in his classic work, *The Pathans*, which reads with such pace and ease that
it is as difficult to disagree with as it is to put down. Sir Olaf continues
to maintain his links with his beloved *Pukhtoonkhwa* (the land of the
Pukhtoons). This little book ventures into the world with a braver heart
knowing that it has his blessings with it.

Akbar S. Ahmed

Pukhto Proverbs

ابئ مړہ شوہ تبہ ئے و شلیدہ

Death is the end of all.

He that dies pays all debts.

SHAKESPEARE

Grandmother died and her fever ended.

ازغے چه تیرہ وی له کومه څایه وی

The Child is father of the Man.

WORDSWORTH

Where does the sharpness of the thorn come from
(but from the time the plant is born).

اسو او دے سو

Oh the month of Asuf you have burnt us.

(Said in late autumn when the weather is changing, the skies clear,
and the sun searingly hot.)

اسونو له ئے نالونه وهل چیندخو هم پنے پورته کړے

This is a predicament into which one could land when keeping up
with the Jones's.

When the horses were being shoed, the frogs also put up their feet.

اصل له خطا نشته کم اصل ته وفا نشته

True blue will never stain.

There is no fault in a noble person while the ignoble person has no fidelity.

اصیل ته اشارت کم اصل ته کوتک

A nod for a wise man and a rod for a fool.

A hint to the noble, a stick for the ignoble.

الف ویلی نه لام زیر لی

Tried to run before he could walk.

Couldn't read 'alif' yet arrived at 'lam'.

الوتے مارغه په لاس نه راځی

It's no use crying over spilt milk.

A bird that has flown from the hand will not return.

اموخته بلا په بسم الله نه ځی

The gods help them that help themselves.

AESOP

Habitual troubles cannot be prevented by reciting the holy creed alone.

اوبو آخستے خلی ته لاس اچوی

A drowning man will catch at a straw.

Even a straw is clutched at when drowning in water.

اوچو سره لونده هم سوزی

With the dry some wet is also burnt.

اور له راغله دَ کور میرمن شوه

He who lets one sit on his shoulders shall have him presently on his head.

She came to ask for fire and become the mistress (of the house).

اوږے د دَودئ تپارے اوری

A hungry person hears the sounds of the bread being prepared.

اوسپنه په اوسپنه غوخیری

Diamonds cut diamonds.

Iron cuts iron.

اوبښ ته چا وئیل لوړه ښه ده که ژوره وے وئیل چه تو لعنت په دواړو

Six of one and half a dozen of the other.

Someone asked a camel: 'Is ascending good or descending?'
The camel replied: 'May both be cursed!'

اول اوخوره د ځان غوښے بیا اوخوره دَ ښکار غوښے

First deserve, and then desire.

No pains, no gains.

First eat your own meat and then eat the meat from game.

اول دَ نوک خَائے شی بیا دَ خوک خَائے شی

Give him an inch and he'll take an ell.

First let there be place for a nail and then for a fist.

اے پہ شیش محل کښے ناسته بل پہ کانرو مه اوله

People who live in glass houses should never throw stones.

باران پہ تیراه اوشو خر ئے دَ اکبر پورے یووړو

It rained in Tirah and the donkeys of Akbarpura were carried away.

باران نه تښتیدم دَ ناوے لاندے م شپه شوه

They who shun the smoke often fall into the fire.

ITALIAN PROVERB

Escaping from the rain I spent the night under an open drain.

باره دِ لا لیدلے نه ده او پرتوګ ورته دَ دے خُایه اوباسے

Don't cross the bridge till you come to it.

*You have not even seen the Bara river yet and are
already removing your trousers (to cross it).*

برخے تولے ازلی دی - نه په زور نه په سیالی دی

For will in us is over-rul'd by fate.

MARLOWE

One's share is predestined and neither altered by force nor by competition.

بل ته کوهے مه کنه پخپله به په کنِں اوغورزیرے

He falls into the pit who leads another into it.

SPANISH PROVERB

Evil begets evil.

Don't dig wells for others for you will fall into one yourself.

بنده اوترل بارونه - خدائے کول خپل کارونه

Man proposes but God disposes.

THOMAS A KEMPIS

While man was busy securing his load, God implemented His own schemes.

بنده حيران خدائے مهربان

God comes at last when we think he is farthest off.

When man is perplexed God is beneficent.

بنده دَ بنده رحمان دے - بنده دَ بنده شیطان دے

Man is man's own salvation or damnation.

Man is man's own Benefactor; man is also man's own Devil.

بنده یو نور جامه ئے سل نوره

Clothes maketh a man.

For the apparel oft proclaims the man.

SHAKESPEARE

Though man has one appearance, his clothes have a hundred varieties.

بیرئ هم تیاره ده او دودئ هم تیاره ده

The ass between two bundles of hay.

The boat is ready to sail and the food ready for eating.

بیزه د مرکه پټیده د قصاب کره ئې شپه شوه

Out of the frying pan into the fire.

The goat hiding from death passed the night in the butcher's house.

بے کودره مه کدیږه

Look before you leap.

Do not enter the water if there is no ford.

پاکه بی بی وار کړی ناپاکه پر تلوار کړی

Fair and softly go far.

The most cautious passes for the most chaste.

SPANISH PROVERB

Reflection insures safety, precipitancy regret.

ARABIC PROVERB

A chaste lady will be patient while an unchaste one will be hasty.

پخپل کور میرے هم زوره ور وی

A cock crows loudest on his own dunghill.

Even an ant is brave in its own home.

پرے که اوسوزی خو ول هغسے په کنں وی

A burnt rope does not lose its twist.

پښتانه په لنډه لار مړه دی

Pukhtoons love short cuts (though fatally dangerous).

پښتون سل کاله پس بدل واغست وئیل چه زر م واغست

Revenge of a hundred years has still its sucking teeth.

ITALIAN PROVERB

Revenge is sweet.

The Pukhtoon who took revenge after a hundred years said, I took it quickly.

پنځه ګوتے یو شان نه دی

All people differ; usually greatly.
For men most differ as Heaven and Earth.
But women, worst and best, Heaven and Hell.

TENNYSON

Even the five fingers of the hand are not alike.

په پښتنه سرے هندوستان ته هم رسی

Seek, and ye shall find.

THE BIBLE

By enquiring, one can reach India.

په حرکت کښے برکت دے

Nothing venture, nothing win.

Help yourself, and heaven will help you.

LA FONTAINE

There is blessing in action.

په خوله الله په زړه کښ غلا

A fair face, a foul heart.

There's daggers in men's smiles.

SHAKESPEARE

God in the mouth but theft in the heart.

په درنو دروند په سپکو سپکه

Take the tone of the company that you are in.

STANHOPE, EARL OF CHESTERFIELD

*To the heavy (respectable) you are respectable and
to the light (worthless) you are worthless.*

KHUSHAL KHAN KHATTAK (attributed).

په سلو مِ مر کے، په یوه مِ پر مه کے

Death before dishonour.

(Oh God) kill me by a hundred (men) but let me not be shamed for one.

په ښځه ، په آس او په توره ښه اعتبار دے

Four things greater than all things are—
Women and Horses and Power and War.

KIPLING

What reliance is there on a woman, a horse, or a sword.

په کلی غلبله شوه دَ دِم دَ نائ ښه شوه

It is an ill wind that blows nobody good.

*There was a hullabaloo in the village but the barber and the drummer
benefitted from it.*
*(Death or such recurring crises affect the village status quo and only the
lower social orders are said to profit by them.)*

په لاس ورے ښه دے نه په کال غوندے

A bird in the hand is worth two in the bush.

CERVANTES

One ear of corn in the hand is better than a pannier full a year later.

په لیلیٰ هر سرے میئن دے سخ دَ هغو چه لیلیٰ شوه پرِ میئنه

Yet to be loved makes not to love again.

TENNYSON

Although everyone loves Laila, good fortune is only with that man
whom Laila loves.

په منډه نه ده په تنډه ده

The race is not to the swift, nor the battle to the strong but time and
chance happeneth to them all.

THE BIBLE

It is not the running around but that which is written on the forehead
(or in one's luck).

پیاز دِ وی خو په نیاز دِ وی

Better is a dinner of herbs where love is, than a stalled ox and
hatred therewith.

THE BIBLE

The onions you serve with affection have value.

پیر نه الوزی خو مریدان ئے الوزوی

Don't judge the master by the servant's praises.

RUSSIAN PROVERB

Though the pir himself does not fly, his disciples would have him fly.

پیشو دَ غوښے څوکیداره شوه

Who will watch the watchman?

He did not know that a keeper is only a poacher turned outside in,
and a poacher is a keeper turned inside out.

KINGSLEY

The cat became the chowkidar of the meat.

تر ورخ تیرے اوبه بیرته نه جاروزی

The past cannot be recalled.
One thing is certain, that Life flies;
One thing is certain, and the Rest is Lies;
The Flower that once has blown for ever dies.

OMAR KHAYYAM

Water that has passed through the dyke will not return.

تشه لاسه ته مِ دښمن ئے

For Satan finds some mischief still
For idle hands to do.

WATTS

(Oh) empty hand you are mine own enemy.

تنزریه خپلے خولے نیولے

Oh partridge your own mouth (voice) has given you away (to the fowler).

تور په صابن نه سپینیږي

Can the Ethiopian change his skin, or the leopard his spots?

THE BIBLE

Black cannot be made white with soap.

توره په کتو ده او غشے په ویشتو دے

The proof of the pudding is in the eating.

The quality of the sword is in its appearance and that of an arrow
in its striking power.

توره دَ لاله وهی نمرے دَ عبدالله وهی

One beats the bush another catches the hare.

The cat steals the rice and the dog comes and eats it.

CHINESE PROVERB

Lala wields the sword while Abdullah eats the results.

چار محکمه زړه محکمه

He who hast done his duty let him ask for no other happiness.

CARLYLE

Perfect work makes a satisfied heart.

چاره که دَ سرو شی په خیټه دَ منډلو نه ده

Even if it is a golden knife it is not meant to be jabbed into the stomach.

چرته چه ډب وی هلته ادب وی

Spare the rod and spoil the child.

A pet lamb makes a cross ram.

Where there is discipline there is social order.

چرته چه زړه خِی هلته پښے خِی

Home is where the heart is.

Where your heart goes there your feet will go.

چرګ خو یو مارغه دے چه چا اونیوو دَ هغه دے

Might is right.

Possession is nine-tenths of the law.

A cock belongs to the one who catches it.

چرگ له دَ دوک داغ بس دے

A hot skewer is enough (pain) for a chicken.

چه اختیار دَ جنگ لری پښتنه په سنگ لری

He who has the discretion to fight lays conference aside.

چه آسمان ته توکی په مخ ئے را پریوزی

He who spits above himself will have it all in his face.

SPANISH PROVERB

چه اوښان ساتے دروازے سترے ساته

A great ship asks deep waters.

Large fowls will not eat small grain.

CHINESE PROVERB

Those who would keep camels should also have high gateways.

چه اوږه نه خوری بوئ تر نه ځی

He who does not eat garlic will not stink of it.

چه باد نه وی بوټی نه خوزی

There is no smoke without fire.

If there is no wind the bush does not sway.

چه بد کرځے بد به پرځے

Evil begets evil.

چه پخپله ځان ته خان وائ خان نه دے

Self-praise is no praise.

He who praises himself befouls himself.

ITALIAN PROVERB

Who calls himself a Khan is not a Khan.

چه پلار ئے برگ وی نو خُوئ ئے تګ وی

Like father like son.

A chip off the old block.

If the father is a scoundrel the son will also be a scoundrel.

چه پوزه ئے څاخی بلا ترِ پاشی

When the nose runs the ghost rises.

چه په خُان کښ وینی په جهان کښ وینی

The soul is the mirror of the world.

What you see in yourself is what you see in the world.

چه په سر دِ درد نه وی داغ پرِ مه ږده

Never trouble trouble till trouble troubles you.

If there is no pain in your head, don't try to cure it.

چه په سر ئے چاره شی خدائے په زره شی

The devil was sick, the devil a monk would be.

RABELAIS

You learn to pray in misfortune and forget it in good fortune.

RUSSIAN PROVERB

Only when the dagger is over his head does God enter his heart.

چه په گوړه مری په زهرو ئے مه وژنه

Subtlety is better than force.

He who can be killed by sugar should not be killed by poison.

چه په گیدر پسے اوزئے نو تابیا دَ امزری کوه

Be prepared.

When you hunt a jackal be ready to meet a lion.

چه پیسے وی نو ښځه دَ کلابت نه راځی

When there is money the woman will even come from Kalabat.

(A story has it that a poor suitor from Swabi was refused his fiancée from Kalabat [in Hazara]. However, he earned his fortune in India and when his prospective father-in-law arrived with the marriage party he quoted this matal.)

چه پیسے لری لوئ (پټو) له کابله ورته را درومی

Who has wealth will get 'loi' (a fine woollen blanket) from Kabul.
(An example of conspicuous consumption.)

چه تر یو ولے توپ کړے بله آسانه شی

Practice makes perfect.

A novice at the first attempt, an adept at the second.

Chinese proverb

When one jumps over one stream the next becomes easier.

چه تنگ شی نو په جنگ شی

A cornered rat will fight.

Tread on a worm and it will turn.

He who is cornered will fight.

چه خدائے سړے ساتی نو دَ امزری په خوله کښے هم ساتلے شی

He that is born to be hanged shall never be drowned.

If God wishes to preserve a man, He will keep him safe even
in the mouth of a lion.

چه خدائے کوی هغه به اوشی خو دَ اوښ کونړه تینکه اوتړه

Put your trust in God, my boys, and keep your powder dry.

CROMWELL

Trust in God but tie your camel.

THE HOLY PROPHET OF ISLAM

چه خدائے نه که پیر بابا به څه که

No leaf moves but God wills it.

When God does not wish it, what can even Pir Baba do.

چه خوب راشی نو بالښت نه گوری

When sleep comes one doesn't look for the pillow.

چه چا سره اوسیرے په مذهب دَ هغو اوسه

When in Rome do as the Romans do.

Practice the religion of those you live with.

چه څوک خوب کوي دَ هغوی نر کټی خْیرِیږی

A careless watch invites a vigilant foe.

The buffaloes of those who sleep will bear male calves.

*(The story goes that one of two villagers waiting for their buffaloes to
deliver fell asleep. In the meanwhile the buffaloes gave birth to male and
female calves. A female buffalo is considered more valuable for qualities
such as milk-giving. The villager who was awake therefore promptly
switched his male calf for his companion's female calf. Upon waking an
argument ensued between the two and this matal resulted.)*

چه څومره څادر وی دومره پښے غزوه

Cut your coat according to your cloth.

Stretch your feet according to the length of the sheet.

چه څومره دیر وی - هومره خیر وی

Slow and steady wins the race.

Wisely and slow; they stumble that run fast.

SHAKESPEARE

The slower the better.

چه څه تیر شی هغه هیر شی

Let bygones be bygones.

What has passed is forgotten.

چه څه کرے هغه به ریبے

Whatsoever a man soweth, that shall he also reap.

THE BIBLE

چه دَ سوات مرغ زرین ئے په نظر شو - دَ ختک تنزری اووئیل چه فقیر یم

*When he saw the golden pheasant of Swat the partridge of the
Khattak country said 'I am a beggar'.*

*(The Pukhto words for 'I am a beggar' sound very much like
the call of the partridge.)*

چه دَ دوٗو سره جهګړه شی دَ دریم ګړی ورکنے ښه شی

When two fall out, the third wins.

GERMAN PROVERB

When two quarrel the third one among them benefits.

چه دِ نه پښتی مه ګدیږه

Let well alone.

If you are not asked, do not dance.

چه ډير خاندی ډير به ژاړی

There is a cross to every rosary.

Who laughs long will cry long too.

چه زر پاک وی له اوره ئے څه باک وی

If gold is pure why should it fear fire.

چه ځے ځے آبازو له به راځے

How ever far you wander you will eventually return to Abazai
(from where you started).

چه سل خویه ئے نور وی یو به ئے دَ مور وی

Blood will tell.

At least one habit will be of his mother's even if he acquires a hundred more.

چه ښه کوے ښه به مومے

Do good and you will find good.

چه غر ښورب وی نو غرڅه ئے هم ښورب وی

The wealth of the country is the wealth of the people.

If the mountain is prosperous the mountain goats will also be prosperous.

چه غریږی هغه نه وریږی

Barking dogs seldom bite.

That which thunders does not rain.

چه غلا ئے او شوه نو څوکیدار ئے اوساتلو

Closing the stable door after the horse has bolted.

A stitch in time saves nine.

He kept a watchman after the theft.

چه کوپر یاده وے په کوپر پیښ شے

Speak of the devil, and he is sure to appear.

A hyena is bound to appear if always mentioned.

چه لاړشے تر بلخه درسره ده خپله برخه

Appointment in Samarra.

And, When Fate summons, Monarchs must obey.

DRYDEN

Even if you go to Balkh you take your share of destiny with you.

چه لوړیږی کورئ نړیږی

The higher they rise the farther they fall.

His house will collapse when it gets too high.

چه مړ شه هغه پر شه

Death's day is doom's day.

When I'm dead everybody's dead and the pig too.

ITALIAN PROVERB

Who dies has lost (is the loser).

چه مړ شه هغه ورک شه

Once a man dies he is often banished from memory.

The good is oft interred with their bones.

SHAKESPEARE

This proverb could also suggest that until he is dead a man has not lost;

While there's life, there's hope.

Hope springs eternal in the human breast.

POPE

He who dies is lost (forgotten).

چه نن سپک شی صبا ورک شی

He who hath lost his reputation is a dead man among the living.

SPANISH PROVERB

Who today is disgraced, tomorrow will be lost.

چه ونه زړه شی دَ هرے بلا پر شپه شی

Old age is a disease in itself.

When a tree becomes old every spirit/calamity nests for the night in it.

چه ئے زده کړے په خُوانیٔ - هیر به ئے نه کړے تر پیریٔ

Train up a child in the way he should go: and when he is old,
he will not depart from it.

THE BIBLE

That which is learnt in youth is not forgotten in old age.

چیندخ په لوته سور شه کابل ئ ولیدو

This implies the vainglory of a small man boasting, or claiming to know more than he does. One sense is:

A little learning is a dang'rous thing.

POPE

The frog climbed a clod and said he saw Kabul.

خاورے یو خاورے به شو

Earth to earth, ashes to ashes, dust to dust.

THE BOOK OF COMMON PRAYER

For dust thou art, and unto dust shalt thou return.

THE BIBLE

We are dust and will become dust.

خاوند نوم دَ خدائ دے

Husband is another name of God.

(The word for husband is also used for God. The central role and significance of the male is underlined in this matal.)

خبرے لږے عمل ډیر

Actions speak louder than words.

Little talk, more action.

خپلَ بیا هم خپل وی

Blood is thicker than water.

No man is an Island, entire of itself.

DONNE

If a house be divided against itself, that house cannot stand.

THE BIBLE

A relation is after all a relation.

خپل خپل دی پردی مغل دی

Comrades are comrades but outsiders (strangers) are Mughuls.

خپل عمل دَ لارے مل

As you brew so shall you drink.

Your own deeds are your companions along life's journey.

خپله خوله هم قلا ده هم بلا ده

There is no venom compared to that of the tongue.

A destroyer of man lurks under his tongue, and death resides
between his cheeks.

ARABIC PROVERB

One's own tongue is a place of safety or of calamity.

*(The capacity of the tongue in creating or destroying relationships is
aptly phrased in this Pukhto proverb.)*

خپل هفه دی چه په تنګتیا کښ پکار راشی

A friend in need is a friend indeed.

A relation proves himself by rallying round in times of trouble.

خدایه زور راکپے کبر را مه کپے

Oh God give me strength but not pride.

خدائے خبر چه تره کافر دے

He to whom God gave no sons the devil gives nephews.
           SPANISH PROVERB.

God knows that the uncle is an infidel.

(*The special uncle-nephew relationship seems to exist in other lands as well.*)

خر ځان ته حيران خاوند ئے بار ته حيران

The donkey is worried about himself while the master worries about his load.

خر که حج له لاړ شی حاجي نشی

Once a fool always a fool.

If a donkey goes for the 'haj' (pilgrimage) he will still not become a 'haji'.

خر هميشه بے طمع خائے کښ ولاړ وی

For fools rush in where angels fear to tread.

POPE

A donkey will always be standing in unexpected places.

خر ئے په رشے پورے اوتړلو - او ورته وائ چه مه خوره

An open door may tempt a saint.

The donkey was tied beside a heap of grain and then told not to eat from it.

خیرات پخپل قربات

Charity begins at home.

خُنبتن سپی ته اووئیل او سپی لکئ ته

To pass the buck.

The master spoke to his dog and the dog passed it on to his tail.

 څومره خولې دومره خبرے

As many mouths as many opinions.

څومره خرکے دومره ئے بارکے

As the donkey so the load.

څه چه اوشو هغه اوشو

What's done cannot be undone.

Things past redress are now with me past care.

SHAKESPEARE

What is done has been done.

خه دانے لمد ے څه ژرنده ورانه

The grain is wet and the flour mill out of order too.

څه لاس پنا څه غر پنا

Out of sight, out of mind.

A hand and a mountain hide equally.

(A small hand close to the eyes or a large mountain obliterate the vision equally thus hiding whatever there is on the other side.)

دَ بادشاهانو خوب په ميرتون وی

Uneasy lies the head that wears a crown.

SHAKESPEARE

The sleep of kings is on an ant-hill.

دَ بخښلی آس غاښونه مه ګوره

Never look a gift horse in the mouth.

دَ پروت امزری نه ګرځینده ګیدړ بنه دے

They only live who dare.

An active jackal is better than an inactive lion.

دَ پښتون بدی دَ سرے اور دے

The Pukhtoon's enmity is like a (smouldering) dung-fire.

دَ پیښے نه تیښته نیشته

Que sera sera, what will be, shall be.

MARLOWE

There is no escape from the inevitable.

دَ تنه غشے پیدا کیږی او بنده پر سورے کیږی

How sharper than a serpent's tooth it is
To have a thankless child.

SHAKESPEARE

The offspring produced from one's body in turn pierced it like an arrow.

دَ خَتِکو بخته دَ یوسف کم بخته

The good luck of the Khattaks is the misfortune of the Yusufzai.

(The story goes that when Nadir Shah was encamped at Attock a Yusufzai lad stole some harem clothes. The King suspecting the Khattaks ordered a mass slaughter of that tribe. Upon hearing of this, the culprit admitted his guilt. This proverb is said to have been coined as Nadir Shah turned his wrath on to the Yusufzai.)

دَ چک نه ئے غپ زیات وی

His bark is worse than his bite.

دَ دیوے لاندے تیاره ده

The nearer the church, the farther from God.

BISHOP ANDREWS

There is darkness under the lamp.

دَ زرو قدر په زرگر وی

A wool seller knows a wool buyer.

Only the goldsmith knows the value of gold.

دَ زړه نه زړه ته لار وی

Love begets love.

What comes from the heart, goes to the heart.

COLERIDGE

دَ سپی دَ عمر نه مرگ ښه دے

One crowded hour of glorious life
Is worth an age without a name.

MORDAUNT

Death is better than a dog's life.

دَ کور لور خور کړميز نه وی

This saying is the opposite of the following Biblical quote:

A prophet is not without honour, save in his own country,
and in his own house.

THE BIBLE

The daughter and sister of one's own house are to be cared for.

*(The daughter and sister of the house are not so helpless as
to not be able to clean their running noses; in short they have
a respectable status in their homes.)*

دنیا دَ کمر سورے دے

Life's but a walking shadow.

SHAKESPEARE

Life (wealth) is a cliff's shadow (temporary and shifting).

دنیا دَ هغه ده چه خوری نه چه ساتی

The gown is hers who wears it, and the world his that enjoys it.

The world is his who eats (enjoys) it, not his who saves (and skimps).

دنیا ئے هغه ته ورکړه چه دَ پوزے پاکول ئے نه زده

Fortune, that favours fools.

BEN JONSON

God has given the world to him who has not even learnt to clean his nose.

دَ وطن سپی دَ وطن سویه نیسی

Set a thief to catch a thief.

The local dog catches the local hare.

دولس میاشتے کال گنده ئے پشکال

*Of the twelve months of the year the dirtiest is the 'pashkal'
(mid-summer).*

*(Similar proverbs describe the attributes of the various months
of the year.)*

دَ يو لاس نه پړق نه خيژی

It takes two hands to clap.

راست اوسه په لويه لار کښ ملاست اوسه

Do right and do not fear the Devil.

Common fame is seldom to blame.

If you lead an honest life, you can even sleep on the main highway with impunity.

روغ صورت تل اختر دے

Health is wealth.

Good health means permanent 'Eid'.

زورور نه يا لرے يا غلے

With the strong one, either keep your distance or your peace.

زه دِ بوره یم خو میدان پرینږر دے

The Pukhtoon mother's warning to her son is almost identical to that of the Spartan mother's:

Return with your shield or upon it.
And how can man die better
Than facing fearful odds
For the ashes of his fathers,
And the temples of his gods.

MACAULAY

I would rather be a childless mother than have you desert the field of battle.

زهر په زهرو ځی

Desperate disease require desperate remedies.

GUY FAWKES

Devils must be driven out with devils.

GERMAN PROVERB

Poison goes through poison (as an antidote).

ژرنده که دَ پلار ده خو په وار ده

Who cometh first to the mill, first grindeth.

First come, first served.

The use of the mill is by turn even if it belongs to his father.

سرے يو رنگ جامه ئے دوه رنگه

Fair feathers make fair fowls.

God makes, but apparel shapes.

The dignity of a man is doubled by his clothes.

سلنډه چه څربه شی دَ چوهاړی کره پخپله ورکبره شی

Pride will have a fall.

*When the lizard gets fat, he goes of himself to the sweeper's house
(to be killed).*

سل ورځے دَ تخت که يو ګړئ دَ بخت

An hour's luck is preferable to a hundred days on the throne.

*(Said to be the Emperor Humayun's answer to a courtier on recovering
the Delhi throne.)*

سندا ته رباب وهل

Neither cast ye your pearls before swine.

                                     THE BIBLE

To play the rebab before a he-buffalo.

بنه وئیل بنه دی خو دَ نه وئیلو ساری نه دی

Speech is silver, silence is golden.

Speaking well is fine but it is still not equal to silence.

بنځے له یا کور دے یا کور دے

For a woman either the house or the grave.

عقل له بے عقلو زده کیږی

Wisdom rides upon the ruins of folly.

Learn from the mistakes of others.

Wisdom is learnt from the unwise.

غر په غر نه ورځی - بنده په بنده ورځی

Friends may greet, but mountains never meet.

*One mountain does not go to another, but man goes to
his fellow man (for aid).*

غر ننگ او خور دامان قلنگ او خور

Feuds ate up the mountain, taxes the plain.

(*In the mountains, though free, people were ruined by vendettas based*
on the code of chivalry and tribal rivalries; in the plains
Government taxes crippled them.)

غلبیل پاشی کوزے ته وائ تا کښ دوه سوری دی

The pot calls the kettle black.

The sieve rose and said to the water-pot: 'you have two holes in you'.

غوا که توره ده شوده ئے سپین دی

Judge not a book by its cover.

The black woman's breast gives white milk.

RUSSIAN PROVERB

Though the cow is black, its milk is white.

غوئ حلال نه دے ښانکی په سر ګرځوے

First catch your hare then cook it.

Although the ox has not yet been slaughtered,
you carry the dishes on your head.

کارغه دَ ښارو چال زده کوؤ خپل هم تر هیر شو

The camel that desired horns lost even his ears.

A crow learnt the walk of a mynah and forgot its own.

کبر له زوال دے

Pride goeth before destruction, and an haughty spirit before a fall.

THE BIBLE

Pride has a fall.

کږه خوله په سوک سمیږی

A whip for the horse, a bridle for the ass, and a rod for the fool's back.

THE BIBLE

A crooked mouth will be set right with a blow.

که پیر خس دے مرید له بس دے

*Though of straw, the pir is still sufficient (in charismatic awe)
for his disciple.*

که خس یم دَ تا بس یم

Jack is as good as his master.

The Pukhtoon would concur with this Shakespearean line:

I think the King is but a man, as I am: the violet smells to him as
it doth to me.

SHAKESPEARE

Though I am a mere straw I am sufficient for you.

که دِ دی خوره که د نه وی مره

Here is the realism of the mountains at its starkest:

If you have, eat; if you have not, die.

که غر لوئے دے په سرئے لار ده

No man is above the law.

Though the mountain be high, there will still be a road to its top.

که کور مِ وسوه خندق مِ پوخ شه

Out of evil cometh good.

Though my house was burnt, the wall (embankments) became pukka.

کته دِ له چا اوکړه له خپله وروره؟

To rob Peter to pay Paul.

From whom did you make the profit but from your own brother?

لاس چه مات شی غاړے له ځی

Blood is thicker than water.

Though a tree grows ever so high, its falling leaves return to the root.
CHINESE PROVERB

When the hand breaks it goes to the neck.

لږ خوره تل خوره ډیر خوره زهرو کنډیر خوره

Greed is a curse.

One should eat to live, not live to eat.

MOLIERE

Eat little and eat forever, eat too much and eat poison.

له اجله رومبے مه مره

Never say die.

Don't order the coffin until the corpse lies on the table.
RUSSIAN PROVERB

Cowards die many times before their deaths;
The valiant never taste of death but once.

SHAKESPEARE

Do not die before the appointed time.

له بدے ورځے سرے خر ته هم ماما وائ

Necessity teaches the bear to dance.

RUSSIAN PROVERB.

In bad days a man calls even a donkey his uncle.

له تش لوښي لوئ آواز خیژي

Empty vessels make the most noise.

مار خوړلے دَ پړی نه هم ویریږي

Once bitten, twice shy.

The burnt child dreads the fire.

Those bitten by a snake fear even a rope.

مرگ نه په واړه دے نه په زاړه

Death devours lambs as well as sheep.

Death the leveller.

SHIRLEY

Death is not for the young, nor for the old (but for all).

مړه خيټه فارسي وائ

The full stomach speaks Persian.

(*The luxury of acquiring foreign languages and manners comes
with affluence: it also suggests arrogance.*)

مور که وچه وی دَ خُوئ رودل بائده وی

Every bird must hatch her own eggs.

Though the mother is dry, she must suckle her son.

مه داسے خوږ شه چه خوری دے مه داسے تریخ شه چه توکی دے

You will go most safely in the middle.

OVID

*Do not be so sweet that men will eat you up, nor so bitter
that they will spit you out.*

نمر په ګوته نه پټيږی

Truth will out.

Virtue will not be hidden.

The sun cannot be hidden by a finger.

نه ځېنتن خبر وو او نه سپی غپل هسے غل اوتښتیده

A guilty man starts at shadows.

The wicked flee when no man pursueth.

THE BIBLE

Neither was the master awake nor the dog barking, yet the thief bolted.

نه دَ دین نه دَ سادین

To fall between two stools.

Neither of the faith nor of the farm.

نیستی پاکه بادشاهی ده - دولت مند ئے له لِزّت خبر نه دی

Poverty is a pure sovereignty, the rich man knows not of its delights.

وره خوله لوئے خبرے

Small wit, great boast.

Great boast, little roast.

Small mouth, big talk.

وسله که بار ده خو پکار ده

Though arms are heavy their carrying is essential.

ونه چه لوئیږی اصل ته کږیږی

Just as the twig is bent, the tree's inclined.

POPE

When the tree grows it bends to its own genus.

ونې ته ګوره سوری له ئے ورځه

The tree is known by his fruit.

THE BIBLE

Look at the tree before sitting under its shadow.

ویریا راغلے ویریا تلے

Easy come, easy go.

هر چا ته خپل عقل ښه ليدے شی

Every cock thinks his own crow the loudest.

Everyone sees his own intelligence as the best.

هر چا ته خپل وطن کشمير دے

East, West, home's best.

To everyone his own country is Kashmir.

هغه پښتون نه دے چه دَ نوک جواب په سوک نه ورکوی

Eye for eye, tooth for tooth, hand for hand, foot for foot.

THE BIBLE

He is not a Pukhtoon who does not give a blow in return for a pinch.

هله به زاريږم چه له کاره اوزګاريږم

Business first, friendship afterwards.

I will sacrifice myself for you when I am free from work.

يا به شپيلئ وے يا به ستوان خورے

You can't have your cake and eat it too.

Either you can whistle or eat powdery food.

یا خوار مه وے یا هوشیار مه وے

Where ignorance is bliss
'Tis folly to be wise.

GRAY

Don't be both destitute and wise.

یو خوا ڈانگ دے بل خوا پړانگ دے

Between the devil and the deep blue sea.

On this side the staff, on that side the panther.

یو غم له بله غمه نه شرمیږی

Misery loves company.

When sorrows come, they come not single spies,
But in battalions.

SHAKESPEARE

One sorrow is never shy of another sorrow.

یوه هاوه هغه هم سخا وه

But one egg and that addled too.

Book II

MIZH

A
MONOGRAPH
ON
GOVERNMENT'S RELATIONS
WITH THE
MAHSUD TRIBE

by

EVELYN HOWELL

with a foreword by

AKBAR S. AHMED

Foreword

Evelyn Howell's introduction in 1905 to the Mahsuds, the subject of *Mizh*, was as dramatic as the land and people he writes of. It followed the murder of the previous Political Agent and Howell's subsequent posting out of turn at the young age of twenty-seven as acting Political Agent, South Waziristan.[1] Howell eventually held the highest field post related to the Mahsuds, that of Resident Waziristan from 1924–6. When I met him, sixty years after his arrival in the land of the Mahsuds, in 1965 at Cambridge, where he lived opposite my college, Selwyn, he was still mentally alert and spoke with lively memory of days past on the Frontier. He was preparing for a discourse on Khushal Khan Khattak, the great Pukhto poet, whose poems he has translated.[2] He died a few years later at the great age of ninety-four.

Although written almost half a century ago, *Mizh* is nonetheless an accurate and incisive analysis of the Mahsud tribal social organisation today. Diachronically the author delineates the complex inter-relationship between colonial presence and tribal politics. Indeed, I believe *Mizh* is the major and best-known work extant on the Mahsuds and in the words of Sir Olaf Caroe 'the most penetrating of all tribal studies'. Two points stand out clearly in a reading of *Mizh*: the masterly analysis of social structure and organisation and secondly the generous and genuine respect for the tribesman, his code of honour, and his way of life. It must be underlined that his affection and respect (for instance in the Preface) speak with the voice of sincerity for *Mizh* is a government document for official readership and written by an imperial officer at the highnoon of empire.

Pukhtun society in the North-West Frontier Province may be generally divided into two categories: acephalous, segmentary, egalitarian groups living in low-production zones (that generally coincide with the Tribal Areas)

---

1. O. Caroe, *The Pathans* (Karachi: Oxford University Press, 1977), Appendix D.
2. E. Howell and O. Caroe, *The Poems of Khushal Khan Khattak* (Peshawar: Pashto Academy, University of Peshawar, 1963).

and ranked groups with super—and sub-ordinate social positions inhabiting cultivated and irrigated areas (generally the settled Districts of the NWFP). The foremost symbol in society of the former is that of *nang*, honour, as the fundamental in the latter is *qalang*, taxes and rents.[1] Although a plenitude of literature exists on *qalang* Frontier society there is an acute scarcity of data on *nang* society. The three now classic monographs on *nang* society have been written by political officers who served in the Tribal Areas and are:

1. W. R. H. Merk, *Report on the Mohmands* (Punjab Government Press, 1898).
2. L.W. King, *Monograph on the Orakzai Country and Clans*, (Punjab Government Press, 1900).
3. E. Howell, *Mizh: A Monograph on Government's Relations with the Mahsud tribe* (Government of India Press, 1931).

Of the three major *nang* tribal groups, indeed of all the tribes in the Tribal Areas, perhaps the Mahsuds have been the most independent and intractable to administer. The Mahsuds have been in the front ranks of nationalist freedom fighters over the last hundred years against the imperial presence. Death in the holy war (jihad) against the British meant eternal paradise. Lord Curzon provoked beyond endurance recorded his famous order that there would be no peace in Waziristan, the land of the Wazirs and Mahsuds, until 'the military steam-roller has passed over the country from end to end'.

Indeed I am certain the number of British civil and military officers killed in Waziristan by tribesmen must be some sort of an imperial record. Even the Political Agent, the senior-most official and head of the administration, was not safe. Of the thirty-four Political Agents from 1895, the year the Agency was created, to 1947, the year Pakistan achieved Independence, four were assassinated in Waziristan. Major Dodd was killed after playing tennis in the Political Agent's house at Tank

---

1. A. S. Ahmed, *Millennium and Charisma among Pathans* (Routledge and Kegan Paul, 1976); A. S. Ahmed, *Social and Economic Change in the Tribal Areas* (Karachi: Oxford University Press, 1977); A. S. Ahmed, *Pukhtun Economy and Society: Traditional Structure and Economic Development* (Routledge and Kegan Paul, 1979).

(the incident is described by Howell). I must confess that I still feel a sense of unreality when I recall the gruesome incident while playing tennis on the same courts surrounded by a thick growth of eucalyptus that hang like weeping willows and date trees. The last British Political Agent, Mr Duncan, was killed during a tribal assembly (jirga) at the Sararogha Scouts Fort by a young Mahsud whose father had lost his life fighting the British. He had been advised that if he wished to take revenge, the primary law of the Pukhtun code, he had best get on with it and kill Mr Duncan, for soon there would be no Englishman left and London was a long way from Waziristan. To the credit of the Political Agent's bodyguard (badragga) drawn from Wazir and Mahsud tribesmen, the assassin was shot on the spot. A fifth Political Agent finding Waziristan too much put himself out of his miseries by a shot in the head in 1946. No such assassinations have occurred after Pakistan achieved Independence and I am glad to record that the seventeen Pakistani Political Agents survived their tenure in Waziristan.

The Mahsud is no respecter of people however high or mighty where his two basic principles of life, freedom and identification with Islam, are concerned. Jawaharlal Nehru, idol of the Congress national movement and fresh from his political triumphs in India, learned this to his cost in 1946 at Razmak when he was attacked by Mehr Dil, a Manzai Mahsud. Nehru was touring the Tribal Areas to argue the cause of undivided India. The attack shook Nehru and helped him to make up his mind and concede to the demand of the Muslims for the creation of Pakistan shortly afterwards.

The changes in Mahsud economic and social life since 1947 have been as dramatic as their history. Starting from nil statistics in every government department in 1947 South Waziristan Agency today boasts two colleges, fifteen high schools, thirty-one middle schools, and one hundred and seventy-one primary schools spread over the Agency. Numerous and various development schemes have been launched and are in full swing. Over the last three decades Mahsuds have moved in large numbers from the interior of the Agency to Tank in the settled District of Dera Ismail Khan and acquired property in the town and around it. They have thus become owners of two houses (doa kora). Recently thousands of Mahsuds have gone abroad to the Arab States and regularly remit money home. Hundreds have joined government service and Mahsud officers hold high ranks in government service, such as the Development Commissioner of the North-West Frontier Province and the General in the Pakistan Army (the latter is the grandson of Mehr Dil who attacked Nehru). The spread of education and growth of affluence are expectedly creating alternative models of social behaviour for the Mahsud which in many ways are deviant from their own ideal-type model of *Pukhtunwali*, the code of the Pukhtuns.[1] The deviance clearly implies a conscious departure from the traditional tribal model. The generation of Mahsud maliks who requested Howell to allow them to remain untouched by civilisation and 'be men like our fathers before us' (Preface) have passed away and a new generation with new ideas is replacing it.

The reader is fortunate in *Mizh* for apart from its analytic quality it is also a small literary gem. To date its remaining copies of the 150 published were hidden away from general readership and academic research among dusty and inaccessible offices. For instance such standard works on the Frontier as Barth, F. *Political Leadership among Swat Pathans*, The Athlone Press, 1972; Spain, J. *The Pathan Borderland*, Mouton, 1963; and Miller, C. *Khyber*, Macdonald and Jane's, 1977, do not mention it in their bibliographies. It is thus with a sense of pride that the Tribal Research Cell, Government of NWFP, presents the book to a general readership. I would like to bring on record the support and encouragement in this venture of Mr Jahanzeb Khan, Secretary, Home, Tribal Affairs and Information Department, Government of NWFP.

Dr A. S. AHMED,
Political Agent,
South Waziristan,
Tank, NWFP.

22 December 1978.

---

1. Ahmed, *Pukhtun Economy and Society*.

MIZH

A

MONOGRAPH

ON

GOVERNMENT'S RELATIONS

WITH THE

MAHSUD TRIBE

BY

EVELYN HOWELL,

Resident in Waziristan

1924–1926

Preface

One of the younger Mahsud maliks—it was as a matter of fact
Mehr Dad, Abdullai—once remarked to me in conversation:
'Taso pokh diwal ye, mizh laka danga yi'.[1]

The comparison is an exceedingly clever one and ought to be much truer
than it really is. The custodians of civilisation dealing with barbarians,
besides a superior coherence arising from a superior measure of reliance
one upon another and a superior continuity of policy, ought to enjoy
the advantage which a superior knowledge of all that has gone before
can give. To what extent they do enjoy the first two advantages, any one
who reads these pages can form his own opinion. But so natural is it to
expect at least the third for them that all tribesmen universally believe
their Political Agent to spend a good part of his time entering up in a
mysterious and carefully guarded 'daftar'[2] all the good deeds of each
man amongst them, and the contrary, if any, in a sort of personal and
sectional account.

The Political Agent in charge of every transborder tribe certainly ought
to have such a book. But, so far as my knowledge goes, he nowhere has.
Where records exist, they are so voluminous, as in large measure to defeat
their own object, and in South Waziristan they do not exist. They were
destroyed in 1919. It was in the hope that an account of Government's
dealings with the Mahsuds and of the *res gestae* of the men in whose hands
these dealings lay might to some extent make good this deficiency that
I set about the compilation of this record and as the work grew, I began
to hope that perhaps it might be of interest and even of some use to
frontier officers generally. If so, I am fully rewarded for all the labour
that it has cost.

---

1. 'You are a cemented wall, we are like a "danga"'. A 'danga' is a retaining wall built of
   round boulders without cement or mortar, such as is to be seen round almost every
   field in Waziristan.
2. 'Daftar' in current sense means ledger, the proper meaning of the word.

I spoke above of political officers as the custodians of civilisation dealing with barbarians. Against this definition, if he were to hear it, I am sure that Mehr Dad, or any other intelligent Mahsud malik, would emphatically protest. Their argument, which is not altogether in the sub-conscious plane, may be stated thus—'A civilisation has no other end than to produce a fine type of man. Judged by this standard the social system in which the Mahsud has been evolved must be allowed immeasurably to surpass all others. Therefore let us keep our independence and have none of your "qanun"[1] and your other institutions which have wrought such havoc in British India, but stick to our own "riwaj"[2] and be men like our fathers before us.'

After prolonged and intimate dealings with the Mahsuds I am not at all sure that, with reservations, I do not subscribe to their plea.

I have to add a word of cordial thanks to Mr F. V. Wylie, C.I.E., I.C.S., for help in seeing the proofs through the press.

22 April 1929.   E. B. HOWELL

---

1. Law (and order).
2. Tribal custom.

Chapter I

It was in 1848 that the Punjab was annexed and British rule replaced that of the Sikhs on the frontier. In 1848 the Nawab of Tank—Shah Nawaz Khan, Katti Khel—was a refugee with Malik Fatteh Khan, Tiwana. Herbert Edwardes[1] recalled him and put him in charge of the Tank illaqa and all frontier affairs on the Tank border. Until 1854 he managed them very well and there were few raids. Then his power began to decline and the hill tribes resumed their old habits of plunder.[2] In March 1860 a Mahsud lashkar 3,000 strong attempted to sack Tank town, but was foiled by the military skill of Risaldar Saadat Khan of the 5th Punjab Cavalry. The lashkar was routed and 300 Mahsuds were killed, including six leading maliks, amongst whom was Jangi Khan, Salimi Khel, the father of Umar Khan.

In consequence of the attack on Tank a military expedition was sent against the Mahsuds in 1860 and penetrated Mahsud country. After a stiff fight on the Palosina plain, which took place while a strong column was away at Nanu, Jangi Khan's village, the troops encountered no great opposition till they reached the Barari Tangi, which was forced on 4 May. One column then visited Kaniguram which was held to ransom for Rs. 2,000 and the other destroyed Makin. The force then returned to India *via* the Khaisora, halting one day at Razmak on their way. The Mahsuds made no submission, but the expedition had the usual effect of keeping the tribe in better order for some years afterwards. After the expedition, although control of the border was left in the Nawab's hands, British officers began to take more interest in Mahsud affairs and to deal in some instances more directly with the headmen. In 1865–6 Major Graham (Deputy Commissioner, Dera Ismail Khan) carried through two schemes—one for allotting certain waste lands in the district to the

---

1. Note No. 1 at the end.
2. Note No. 2 at the end.

Mahsuds, and the other for recruiting twenty-five Mahsud horsemen[1] for border service. It was his intention, as the Bahlolzai Mahsuds, especially the Shingis, were the most troublesome marauders, to give the bulk of these favours to them. Tribal sentiment however prevailed and he was compelled to assign them equally among the three main branches of the tribe.[2] So the Shingis only got three horsemen out of twenty-five. Umar Khan, son of Jangi Khan, in the negotiations fully vindicated his position as 'leading Khan of the tribe', Yarik Khan,[3] Langar Khel, and Sarfaraz Khan, Michi Khel, being second and third. The effect of these measures was short lived. Mr Bruce, writing as Deputy Commissioner, Dera Ismail Khan, in 1888, says that in 1867 'the sad and humiliating record of offences committed by the Mahsuds...was resumed and continued without any intermission throughout the years 1867–1872'. Mr Bruce appears to connect this fact with frequent changes in local control. There were as a matter of fact five transfers of the post of Deputy Commissioner, Dera Ismail Khan, in which only four officers were concerned.

In 1873 Captain Macaulay, who had taken over charge of the district in April 1871, assumed direct control of border affairs. This caused the Nawab to sulk and in August 1875, with the permission of the Punjab Government, he retired to Lahore, where he lived until the day of his death in 1882. A letter of Captain Macaulay, dated 9 March 1873, throws much light on subsequent events. By vigorous administration he had secured a number of Mahsud prisoners and was thus able to bring pressure to bear. He distinctly records that 'the three branches of the Mahsuds have always been dealt with separately' ...and consequently 'it would appear hardly less fair at present to hold the Alizais responsible for acts of the Shaman Khels than to hold the Shaman Khels responsible for the acts of the Bahlolzais. The conduct of the Alizais has been esteemed good for the last ten years and they have enjoyed in consequence unbroken intercourse with British territory for that period. The conduct of the Shaman Khels has only been bad on certain occasions and they have been

---

1. Note No. 3 at the end.
2. Note No. 4 at the end.
3. Yarik Khan's sister was married to the Nawab of Tank.

prohibited British territory for the last seven years[1].... The conduct of the Bahlolzais, on the contrary, has been persistently and uniformly bad for the last ten years during which time they have been excluded from British territory'. The occasion of this letter was a settlement effected with the Shaman Khel. To effect the release of their prisoners the Shaman Khel jirga agreed to deposit hostages and pay a fine of Rs. 3,000. The settlement was approved, the fine paid and 'eleven of the most influential maliks and nine of less note' came to Dera as hostages.

In 1874 a similar settlement was effected with the Bahlolzai. They paid a sum of Rs. 7,085 claimed from them as compensation and a fine of Rs. 3,000, and also furnished thirty-three hostages. Of the negotiations with the Bahlolzai Mr Bruce writes 'It is a well-known fact that the final settlement was not concluded either through or with the concurrence of the Nawab. He paid the greater part of the fine of Rs. 5,000 out of his own pocket, and Umar Khan, Yarik Khan and others held themselves entirely aloof'.... 'I can appreciate the advantage it might have been... to assume direct relations with the Wazirs independently of the Nawab of Tank; but I fail to see where the advantage lay in deposing the Nawab and setting up Azim Khan,[2] Kundi, in his room, an ordinary lumbardar who had neither status nor antecedents, or of supplanting Umar Khan from his legitimate position in favour of an adventurer who had no influence beyond that of a petty faction leader like Nabi Khan, Shingi'. This man Nabi Khan's previous history is instructive. In the struggles which preceded the accession of the Amir Sher Ali to the throne of Kabul, a rival claimant, the Sirdar Muhammad Azim Khan, son of the Amir Dost Muhammad by another wife, took refuge in Waziristan. The exile was accompanied by his nephew, the future Amir Abdur Rahman. Nabi Khan gave the fugitives shelter and in return, when his affairs prospered, Muhammad Azim Khan found employment for Nabi Khan at Kabul.

---

1. Their chief offense was committed outside British Territory though against British subjects. It consisted in the murder of 60 Hindus from Tank at a shrine of Shiva Ji near Murtaza in the Gumal. This took place in the year 1868. Chaudhri Badda Ram tells me that he once was taken to this shrine when a boy and he remembers hearing of this incident in his earlier years.
2. In the light of after events, when Azim Khan, Kundi, became Mr Bruce's *alter ego*, the passage is of interest.

On Sher Ali's accession, Nabi Khan was thrown into prison. He escaped and returned to his own country, where his rivalries with Umar Khan for years reflected on a narrower stage, the dynastic squabbles of the Barakzai sirdars.

In 1875 the Bhitannis, Mianis, and Ghorezai were induced to take over Pass responsibility by the distribution amongst them of service allowances—Rs. 11,220 per annum to the Bhitannis and Rs. 3,360 to the other two. These payments were intended by the Punjab Government to be on a sillahdari basis, the payments being actually made to the maliks who nominated the 'bargirs'. But this procedure was apparently never observed.

Major Graham's colonisation scheme of ten years before had broken down, but in pursuance of the same idea it was revived in 1877 at the request of Nabi Khan, Shingi. An expenditure of Rs. 10,000 was sanctioned for the purchase of waste lands near the Gumal Pass on which Mahsuds were to be located and in return were to accept responsibility in respect of the Pass. To the land allotted was to be attached the condition of providing one footman for Pass service for every 100 kanals allotted and one horseman for every 200 kanals. Certain lands had been purchased but had not yet been made over to the grantees, when the famous Tank raid of 1 January 1879, led by Umar Khan, took place. This colonisation scheme was either a *pisaller* or subsidiary to another which Major Macaulay was about this time strongly pressing on his superiors. He proposed to police the Gumal Pass with Mahsud and Wazir levies and in return for the service thus rendered to levy a toll of Re. 0-8-0 per camel and Re. 0-3-0 per bullock on the Powindas using the Pass. He reckoned thus to collect more than enough to pay for the necessary Wazir and Mahsud levies and also to cover the grant of an inam of Rs. 10 per mensem to each of the ten leading maliks in each of the three main branches of the Mahsud tribe. In return he was prepared to surrender the hostages whom he held. This is the first mention of allowances other than maintenance of hostages, sillahdari, or service payments in the history of our dealings with the Mahsuds. It was in connection with this scheme that Major Macaulay went up the Gumal to Khajuri Kach under tribal escort in November 1878. The scheme had once before that time been put forward and rejected out of deference to the Amir's susceptibilities.

It was now (September 1878) revived as one of the war measures approved by Government 'in order to detach from all political connection with the Afghan Government those independent tribes on our border whom it is most important...to bring permanently under our own influence to the exclusion of that of the Amir'. A number of interesting facts are recorded in Major Macaulay's letters. It appears that, profiting by the new system of Pass responsibility, Major Macaulay had felt himself able for the first time in 1877 to deal with the Mahsud tribe as a whole and had put them all under blockade. This was done for the offence of kidnapping a single Hindu child.[1] As a result of six months' blockade, the tribe, in February 1878, submitted unconditionally, and Umar Khan, the leading malik, brought in the innocent cause of their sufferings in his arms, saying 'For God's sake take this curse away from us'. Umar Khan is described by Major Macaulay as not only head of the tribe, but also as leader of the party in the tribe known as the Ahmedzai or the Nawab's party, 'who go to Kabul, are fanatical and ill-disposed and many of them systematically demoralised by being constantly suborned to commit crime in our territory'. Consequently Major Macaulay retained his preference for Nabi Khan,[2] Shingi, and other well-disposed headmen. It was mainly to them that he was proposing to allot the lands which he had purchased, and large numbers of these men, with their families, came down to Tank to secure their share in the lands. In connection with these negotiations the Mahsud hostages had also been allowed to move their families from Dera Ismail Khan to Tank, where there was thus a very large congregation of Mahsuds animated by a lively sense of favours to come.

Excluded from a share, or perhaps what he considered his proper share, in these benefits, it was not unnatural that Umar Khan should show his power. He had been in Kabul while Major Macaulay was traversing the Gumal Pass and absented himself, as also did Yarik Khan, from the subsequent negotiations. Apart from their hereditary influence, these two had small difficulty in collecting a following. For in the years 1877–8 the

---

1. There were other offences, regarded as serious at the time, but this was the only case of kidnapping. Major Macaulay definitely says that the blockade was imposed to compel the restitution of this child.
2. Note No. 5 at the end.

Amir Sher Ali had 'at the instigation of Russia'[1] been spending money amongst the Mahsuds for hostile purposes and had fostered the anti-British faction among the tribe. Umar Khan's attack on Tank was the direct outcome of these activities. Many of the opposite faction no doubt knew what was coming and joined the marauders. Nevertheless Umar Khan's rash though unexpectedly successful move had been taken without the concurrence and against the wishes of the large and influential body of maliks who were expecting the allotment of lands. No less than one hundred and eighty-three of these were actually in Tank with their families when the attack took place. As many of these as were allowed at once surrendered themselves with their families and not a few others from the hills shortly after followed suit. They thus saved themselves from the rigours of the blockade which at the time, in the height of the Afghan War, was the only measure that Government was in a position to take in punishment for the outrage. For more than two years the blockade was maintained and the tribe was reduced to real distress. Pitiful letters to the new Amir of Kabul for the moment produced no result and when, in the spring of 1881, the tribe learnt that, the Afghan War over, Government was preparing an expedition to deal with them, they made a genuine effort. The six ring-leaders of the attack on Tank were:

1. Umar Khan, Salimi Khel, Alizai,
2. Matin, Langar Khel, Alizai,
3. Yarik, Langar Khel, Alizai,
4. Azmat, Shingi, Bahlolzai,
5. Boyak, Aimal Khel, Bahlolzai,
6. Mashak, Abdur Rahman Khel, Nana Khel, Bahlolzai.

The last mentioned was, according to Mr Bruce, not really a tribal malik at all and owed his position entirely to personal qualities. As the surrender of these six men was demanded by Government, they naturally became the leaders of the war party. But the effects of the blockade and the activities of those who had surrendered—for they were allowed to return freely to the hills and there carry on a campaign of counterpropaganda— were too much for them, and in April 1881, before the troops had crossed

---

1. The words are quoted from Major Macaulay's letter No. 120-P., dated 8 October 1881.

the border, four of them had been forced to give themselves up. Of the two who did not so surrender, Yarik, who was ill, sent his son Hashmi in his place, and Mashak came as far as Kot Shingi, where his heart failed him and he turned back.

With the tribe thus divided against itself the troops met with little opposition. One column under General Kennedy, with Major Macaulay as Political Officer, entered Mahsud country *via* Jandola, passed through the Shahur Tangi and up the Shahur as far as Turan China, near the point where it is joined by the Denawat. From here a detached column visited Spli Toi and destroyed Mashak's dwelling and burnt his crops. The force then proceeded across the Barwand Raghza to Nanu and entered the Khaisara, where some opposition was expected, but the hostile gathering was dispersed by Shah Salim, Michi Khel. On its way from the Khaisara to Kaniguram, then a town inhabited almost entirely by Saiyyids and Urmurs, near a place called Shah Alam, the force had something like a battle, in which the Mahsuds lost heavily and Madamir (Nazar Khel), Aimal Khel, the leading hostile in the field, was killed. Thereafter there was scarcely any pretence at opposition and so little sniping that the Political Officers with both columns were able to levy fines of Rs. 50 or 100 for every shot fired at the troops. From Kaniguram General Kennedy's column marched to Makin where it joined hands with General Gordon's force which had come from Bannu up the Khaisora *via* Razani and the Razmak Narai to Razmak, where it was encamped. Mr Udny (Deputy Commissioner, Bannu) accompanied this force as Political Officer. It scarcely fired a shot the whole time. Survey parties accompanied by maliks ascended Kundi ghar, Pre Ghal, and Shuidar. Supplies were freely brought in everywhere and liberally paid for, fines being deducted from the sums paid. The two columns withdrew unmolested—one down the Takki Zam and the other by the Shaktu—and were back in British India by the middle of May.

Scarcely were the troops out of the country when a dramatic and, till then unprecedented, event occurred. An emissary from the Amir, one Mazullah Khan, Durani, appeared in Kaniguram, and offered a renewal of the Amir Sher Ali's subsidies. Although the nature of his reception was such that he did not stay long, Mazullah Khan's appearance did not fail to delay compliance with the conditions imposed. When he left in July

Yarik, Mashak and a son of Umar Khan went with him. After they were gone it became known to the tribe at large that offers of allegiance to the Amir in their names had been made, and one Daulat Khan, Shingi, set about recruiting 1,000 Mahsuds for service under the Afghans. A strong reaction followed and Daulat Khan was handed up to the British. This was not long in becoming known at Kabul. Indeed the Mahsuds sent a letter to the Amir asking him to mind his own business. Those who accompanied Mazullah accordingly met with a cool reception and returned disappointed. On their arrival in Mahsud country, Yarik surrendered voluntarily and Mashak was brought down to Tank bound hand and foot and made over to the police.

This was the most complete act of submission that the Mahsuds have ever done, before or since. It was accompanied by complete acceptance of the Government terms. These were:

1. a fine of Rs. 30,000 for the attack on Tank;
2. payment of compensation for that and other offences to the amount of Rs. 72,947. Of these sums about Rs. 10,000 were shown as recovered by the troops during the expedition. This recovery was effected by cutting the green crops of notorious hostiles for fodder without payment;
3. a tax of 1/4 on all Mahsud bahirs, which were restricted to the Gumal and Takki Zam routes, in order to recover the balance due from the tribe;
4. the maintenance of eighty Mahsud hostages at a monthly cost of Rs. 1,000. The hostages were to be invested by the tribe 'with the character and power of "chalweshtas" whose functions are to carry out the wishes and decisions of the tribal council'. Major Macaulay described this proposal (*i.e.* the investment of the hostages with the position of chalweshtas) as an experiment which at worst could do no harm.

As has been shown, for historical reasons, there had only hitherto been Shaman Khel and Bahlolzai hostages. By admission of its strongest advocate, Major Macaulay, the hostage system had 'never at any period exercised any direct and practical effect in curbing the criminal tastes and habits of their tribe'. But he and others believed the educative effects of living in British India to be very valuable and 'what was originally viewed as a penalty began to be contested for as a prize', to be divided according to recognised tribal shares. This characteristic inversion had important consequences later on. Government at the same time also gave its approval to the revival of the Gumal Pass and colonisation schemes.

It has been mentioned how at a very early stage Mahsuds had been admitted to border service. In course of time the twenty-five Mahsud sowars had somehow come to be replaced by eight sowars at Rs. 20 p.m. each, and thirteen footmen at Rs. 8 p.m. each. These men were on a sillahdari basis and actually received—a sowar Rs. 10 and a footman Rs. 5 p.m.—the balance being paid to the maliks who nominated them. This principle of division of the whole sum of Rs. 264 p.m. was introduced by Major Macaulay himself.

'It appears, however, that he afterwards allowed this essential principle to be disregarded, and individuals were enlisted who paid no "sillahdari" to the maliks and were entertained without any reference to them. Subsequently another change was made in the distribution, the sowars being paid Rs. 12-8-0 and the footmen Rs. 7 each p.m.'

In spite of this omission for some years after the expedition of 1881 the Mahsuds, having had their lesson and not being further disturbed by intrigues from Kabul, behaved well.

Consequently in 1884 the four imprisoned ringleaders who were still alive were released. Meanwhile, in 1882, Mr Thorburn had replaced Major Macaulay as Deputy Commissioner, Dera Ismail Khan. This officer reported that the arrangement proposed for the recovery of the fine was working very slowly and was killing Mahsud trade, and that the chalweshta system was a hopeless failure. But the revised arrangements which he proposed for spending the amount sanctioned for the tribe, *viz.* Rs. 1,264[1] p.m., were not approved and for some years nothing was done. The Mahsud colonisation scheme continued to be a failure and, by the standards of those times, a costly failure. During the winter of 1887–8, Mr Ogilvie being then Deputy Commissioner, Dera Ismail Khan,

---

1. Rs. 1,000 for hostages and Rs. 264 for service.

an attempt was made to send a Survey Expedition up the Gumal under tribal escort as a first step towards the opening of the Pass, under arrangements similar to those proposed by Major Macaulay. Owing to disputes between the Mahsud, Zilli Khel Wazir and Powinda maliks who accompanied the party, the attempt failed and in February 1878 the expedition was withdrawn *re infecta*. An expenditure of Rs. 14,000 had been incurred and an additional Rs. 3,500 was paid as compensation. In consequence of this failure the Mahsud hostages were, in April 1888, dismissed. Incidentally we learn that in 1889 of the fine imposed in 1881 Rs. 65,000 were still unrecovered.

Early in 1888,[1] Mr Bruce replaced Mr Ogilvie as Deputy Commissioner and Mr Ogilvie became Commissioner. Mr Bruce at once set to work and during the summer of 1888, acting without full authority, made a new settlement with the tribe, upon terms which his superior officers considered to be unduly soft. The chief features of this were that:

1. the tribe made some sort of amends (by paying up Rs. 1,790 in cash) for the twenty offences 'most of them more or less serious and some very bad'[2] committed during the summer of 1888, after the dismissal of the hostages;
2. they gave a bond with Azim Khan, Kundi, as surety for the payment of the sum of Rs. 3,500 above mentioned;
3. they surrendered two Marwat outlaws, whom they had sheltered.

In return instead of re-establishing the hostage system the tribe received its allowances of Rs. 1,264 p.m. in return for service on the border, and a list was drawn up showing the distribution of this amount among the chief maliks of the three main branches on a sillahdari basis. The sillahdars were sixty-one in number, of whom twenty-seven were Bahlolzai, and seventeen each from the other two branches. Mr Bruce did not defend this Bahlolzai preponderance, except on the ground that the Bahlolzai had had more than their share of the hostages and of the old sillahdari arrangements. Hostages had been in the first instance taken from those sections which gave trouble. The punishment had come in course of time

---

1. Note No. 6 at the end.
2. Fifty-three offences were recorded. They were mostly petty cattle raids.

to be regarded as a favour. Thus was perpetuated, or at least prolonged, the principle, traces of which may still be seen in the division of the Mahsud allowances, *viz.*, that those who give most trouble get most reward. These lists of sillahdars were attested by fifty-one maliks and Mr Bruce states that he now knew who the real representative men of the tribe were, and had satisfied himself that the fifty-one comprised all the leading men of note in the tribe. They had been accepted as such by all the minor maliks in full jirga and authorised to answer for the tribe. The Commissioner on this claimed that 'for the first time in the history of our dealings with the Mahsud tribe, it appears that substantial progress has been made towards the formation of a manageable representative jirga on a sound basis'.

The same claim may have been put forward before. It has certainly been so since, more than once, but the desired result has not so far been accomplished.

Chapter II

The new settlement was obviously both in Mr Bruce's mind and that of the
Mahsuds only a preliminary step. Major Macaulay's scheme for opening
the Gumal Pass had now been in the air for ten years or more, and the
Mahsuds, in characteristic fashion, had convinced themselves that, if it
were adopted, they were to receive service payments and allowances to the
amount of Rs. 25,000 per annum. This money they were of course eager
to finger. Mr Bruce on his side was convinced that what had been done
by Sir R. Sandeman and himself in Baluchistan could also be done in
Waziristan and should be done there. The Commissioner shared his views,
though he did not altogether like the terms of Mr Bruce's settlement. The
local officers, after much discussion, verbal and written, convinced the
Punjab Government and that Government in turn, according a somewhat
grudging approval to the settlement, recommended the Gumal scheme
to the Government of India. Consequently in November 1889 the
Viceroy (Lord Lansdowne), accompanied by the Commander-in-Chief,
the Lieutenant-Governor of the Punjab, and Sir R. Sandeman, Agent
to the Governor-General in Baluchistan, made a tour in the Derajat,
during the course of which, after numerous conferences of high officials,
His Excellency too was converted. Action followed promptly. An
annual expenditure of Rs. 50,000 was sanctioned for the Gumal tribes
('Waziris and Sheoranis') and of Rs. 25,000 for the Mando Khel of Zhob.
In return it was expected that Rs. 17,000 would be realised from tolls.
In January 1890 a great jirga was held by Sir R. Sandeman at Appozai
(since known as Fort Sandeman) at which Mr Bruce was also present.
The jirga was largely attended by maliks of the tribes concerned and
was pronounced a great success. Government's proposal was explained
to the tribal representatives assembled and accepted by them.[1] On
their acceptance the unrecovered balance of the fine imposed on the
Mahsuds in 1881 (Rs. 65,000) was remitted and distribution lists for the

---

1. Note No. 7 at the end.

disbursement of the sanctioned sums were drawn up. Simultaneously the Amir was informed by the Governor-General that the Gumal scheme was of strategic and political benefit to the British Government and therefore to be blessed, that it was nevertheless no menace to himself and was anyhow none of his business. The correspondence which I have seen does not show whether His Highness returned any direct reply to this missive.

No time was lost in giving effect to at least a portion of the sanctioned scheme. No tolls were levied from Powindas using the Pass and no revenue therefore accrued to meet the enhanced expenditure, but posts of a kind were at once built for tribal levies at Spinkai, Nili, and Khajuri Kach and the Pass was used, without untoward incident, on several occasions during 1890–1, for the passage of bodies of troops and civil officials. In May 1892 came the Amir's rejoinder. Sirdar Gul Muhammad Khan, an Afghan official, appeared in Wana with a force of 100 cavalry and the same number of infantry and started to persuade the Mahsuds and Darwesh Khel Wazirs to sever all connection with the British Government and accept allegiance to the Amir. One of the Sirdar's emissaries, Khalifa Nur Mohammad, even penetrated as far as Jandola with a similar message to the Bhitannis. By the Sirdar's appearance the Mahsud tribe was at once divided into factions—pro-Afghan and pro-British; and the former could think of no better means of distinguishing themselves than by acts of hostility against Government. There was therefore a marked increase of offences committed by the Mahsuds during the summer of 1892. It was at the request of the pro-British maliks that troops were accordingly moved up in August to Jandola[1] and to Khajuri Kach. The Sirdar and his followers then withdrew. It is perhaps significant that it was close upon the heels of this episode that the Durand Mission was sent to Kabul. It resulted, in November 1893, in the conclusion of an agreement by which the Durand Line was fixed and the Amir accepted that line as the eastern limit of his influence. Meanwhile however, for the time being, the mischief had been done. A fine of Rs. 9,000 was indeed imposed on the Mahsuds for their misdeeds of 1892, but as soon as the troops at Jandola were reduced, and those at Khajuri Kach withdrawn, the tale of crime began again on the borders of British India, in the Gumal and in Zhob. It was in Zhob that Mr Kelly of the Public Works Department

1. Regulars have ever since remained at Jandola until 1924.

was murdered by two Abdur Rahman Khel Mahsuds named Jambil and Karam, both of whom appear amongst the Bahlolzai signatories of the Appozai agreement. A sowar of the regular cavalry was murdered about the same time near Zam Post, and a few months later four regular sepoys near the Ghwaleri Kotal in the Gumal Pass. The last mentioned offence was attributed to some Nekzan Khel assisted by Shakaiwal Wazirs, and it was settled in the usual manner by fine and security. But of the other two offences more serious note was taken. The murder of the cavalry sowar was known to be the work of three Abdullais, instigated by a malik named Shahir who, on Mr Bruce's showing, was 'bitterly discontented about inequalities which occurred in the distribution of the service allowances—made at Fort Sandeman in 1899'. He had as a matter of fact got nothing there. By means of barampta, stoppage of allowances, and the exercise of his personal influence Mr Bruce was able, after very prolonged negotiation, to secure the surrender for trial by jirga and imprisonment, if convicted, of the five actual criminals above named,—a very remarkable achievement. After surrender they were tried and duly convicted. The two Abdur Rahman Khel were sentenced to seven years, and the three Abdullais to two years' imprisonment *plus* a fine of Rs. 5,000 or an additional five years in default. But the success was illusory. The opposition, amongst whom Mulla Powinda of the Sultanai Shabi Khel now first comes into prominence, retaliated against the maliks chiefly instrumental in effecting the surrender. Three were murdered, two driven out of the country, and 'the rest went about in peril of their lives'.[1] Already in 1892 the practice of civil officers moving about under tribal escort 'north of the Gumal and in other tracts in Waziristan' had been prohibited by Government. On this further manifestation of opposition the Punjab Government, with a glimpse of real insight into the essentials of the Sandeman system, actually recommended that a punitive expedition should be undertaken to punish the offenders. But the Government of India, busy with their schemes of frontier demarcation arising out of the Durand Agreement, turned a deaf ear. Mr Bruce was 'instructed to continue his communications with the tribal jirgas, with the object of procuring, if possible, the punishment of the murderers of the maliks by the tribes themselves'. Naturally enough nothing came of these

---

1. Note No. 8 at the end.

communications. So perished the application of the Sandeman policy to Waziristan. But neither Mr Bruce, its chief exponent, nor apparently any one else, seems to have realised or at least, represented, that whatever they were doing, it was no longer the Sandeman policy on which they were working. Mr Bruce had been selected as British Commissioner for the delimitation of a portion of the frontier and in connection therewith a further expenditure of one lakh of rupees per annum was sanctioned for:

1. the opening up of the Tochi and Gumal trade routes into Afghanistan,
2. removing inequalities in the Wazir and Mahsud distribution list,
3. the prevention of raids into Zhob,
4. obtaining reparation in outstanding cases.

Simultaneously Government decided on the permanent occupation of Wana, and for Wana Mr Bruce started in October 1894 with a strong escort of troops. On reaching Karab Kot he received letters from Mulla Powinda pressing for the release of the Abdullai and Abdur Rahman Khel prisoners, and insisting that troops should not be located at Wana. Mr Bruce sent a verbal reply declining to communicate with the Mulla except through the tribal maliks. What followed is a matter of common knowledge. A lashkar of about 2,000 Mahsuds attacked and a party of their swordsmen penetrated the camp at Wana some hours before dawn on 3 November, and was with difficulty ejected after severe fighting. The terms demanded by Government in reparation for this unprovoked attack were:

1. the surrender as hostages of the eighteen leaders,
2. the expulsion of Mulla Powinda until demarcation was complete,
3. restoration of all rifles, horses, and money taken, or reparation at the rate of Rs. 500 for every missing rifle or horse.

The friendly maliks, aided by the friends of Government amongst the Wazirs, Dotannis, and Powindas, soon persuaded the Mulla to dismiss his lashkar, and the tribal jirga, with two representatives of the Mulla, returned to Wana. The jirga agreed to try to comply with the terms, but failed to do so within the allotted time.

Consequently on 18 December 1894 Mahsud country was, for the third time, invaded by the forces of the British Government. Great stress had been laid on the importance of preventing the expedition 'from developing into one against whole tribes.' The only way in which this could be done that Mr Bruce could suggest was for the friendly maliks to accompany the different columns and perform the usual miscellaneous services. In the absence of any more palatable proposal this was reluctantly accepted by the General Officer Commanding (Sir William Lockhart), who was also invested with supreme political control. The Abdullai and Shabi Khel, especially those of Torwam, which had been the final rendezvous of the Mulla's lashkar, the Abdur Rahman Khel, the Garrarai of Ahmadwam, and certain Langar Khel sections were regarded as the chief culprits to be punished. But the troops did not confine themselves solely to this task. It was also thought desirable that columns should visit as much of Mahsud country as possible, and objectives were fixed:

- for the first Brigade (which was already at Wana) Kaniguram—*via* the Tiarza and Shorawangi algads;
- for the second Brigade, from Jandola, Makin *via* the Takki Zam;
- for the third Brigade, from Bannu, Razmak *via* the Khaisora.

All three columns reached their respective points, with little or no opposition, simultaneously on 21 December and set about their task of destroying the houses and towers, and capturing the flocks of the opposition and exploring the country. As in 1881 there was little or no fighting and 'Waziristan was traversed from one end to the other'. The amount of damage inflicted on the enemy was assessed by the Mahsuds themselves at about Rs. 1.5 lakhs, and the estimate was considered to be not far out.

As the condition of peace the surrender as hostages of eighteen men, ring-leaders of the attack on the troops at Wana, as well as restoration in kind or cash of all property looted at Wana, and the payment of a fine of nearly Rs. 13,000, due over outstanding cases, had been demanded. There were also two other demands, *viz.*, the opening of the Shahur route to Wana and the exclusion of Mulla Powinda until the delimitation of the Indo-Afghan boundary was complete. By the end of February 1895 all these, even the surrender of the hostages, had been accepted or fulfilled.

Garrisons of regular troops, intended to be permanent, were retained at Jandola and Wana, and a force was left encamped at Barwand,[1] the open plain to the north of Sarwakai, to keep the Shahur route to Wana open. Of these only the force at Barwand was in Mahsud country, the rest of which had been evacuated even before the terms were fully complied with. To Barwand Mr Bruce, who on the break up of the force had once more been put in chief political control of Waziristan, repaired early in March and there, no doubt, he elaborated his proposals for a new settlement with the Mahsuds which he submitted to Government in May. Mr Bruce had now (1895) been for seven years, first as Deputy Commissioner, Dera Ismail Khan, and then as Commissioner of the Derajat Division, in close contact with the Mahsuds, and if ever any Englishman could claim to know them well, Mr Bruce was the man. The substance of his scheme was to increase the Mahsud allowances from Rs. 51,228[2] to Rs. 61,548 per annum. This Mr Bruce considered necessary, both on general grounds, because judged by the Baluchistan standard the amount paid was incommensurate with the responsibilities undertaken by the recipient maliks, and also to redress the individual grievances of those who had come off badly in the Appozai distribution of 1891. Mr Bruce frankly admitted that there had been flaws in the earlier distribution, due to his then imperfect knowledge of the tribe. The errors of deficiency he proposed to correct, but he said nothing about the errors of excess, of which there must also have been some. The amount which he now suggested was in effect the same that he had asked for five years earlier, when he had been limited to Rs. 50,000, and he obviously hugged the idea, as so many of his successors have done since, that could just a little more money be granted, the perfect distribution list would be achieved and all future trouble disappear. This idea—to leave the narrative for a moment—is and must always be an illusion. To begin with, the rapacity of the Mahsuds is insatiable; to go on with, tribal society is not static, and a list that is perfect today will be imperfect next week; finally, the distribution list is regarded as a warrant of precedence, and no race of men that ever yet existed has ever been reasonable over questions of precedence, as perhaps the records of other hills besides

---

1. Note No. 9 at the end.
2. The excess over Rs. 50,000 was unsanctioned and paid with contingencies.

those of Waziristan could testify. Be that as it may, Mr Bruce prepared a very elaborate and careful[1] list of maliks, graded in five classes according to the measure and extent of their influence. This list has been the basis of many subsequent distributions, and was probably more nearly perfect than any of them. On the one hand then the Mahsuds were to receive an additional Rs. 10,000 a year, Rs. 8,000 of which were to go to levies stationed at posts[2] on the Shahur line. On the other hand, the obligations which Mr Bruce, a true disciple of Sir Robert Sandeman, proposed that they should undertake were:

1. general good behaviour;
2. prevention of raids in British India and 'protected areas, such as the Gumal, Wana, Spin and Zarmelan';
3. the surrender for trial and punishment of all tribesmen guilty of offences against Government or against those acting under or in support of Government authority;
4. the furnishing of tribal escorts to officers visiting any part of their country under the orders of Government;
5. rendering the services for which they received allowances in any part of their country according to the convenience of Government.

These of course were in addition to those permanent or continuing conditions which the tribe had accepted as part of the terms of peace. Mr Bruce also advocated the retention of the Barwand force permanently where it was, or in that neighbourhood, and the formation of a strong central cantonment 'at Razmak or some equally suitable central position, with outposts at Sheranna and Wana, to dominate Mahsuds, Darwesh Khels and Dauris'. Government sanctioned the new allowances conditionally on the acceptance by the tribe of Mr Bruce's proposals. At the same time they distinctly forbade him 'ever without their express sanction to act on the offer of the tribe to provide escorts' and declared 'interference of this kind with the interior of Waziri country and the establishment of military posts as sketched by Mr Bruce to be contrary to the existing orders of Her Majesty's Government'. In the same correspondence occurs the first mention of recruiting Mahsuds

---

1. Note No. 10 at the end.
2. Haidari Kach Tangi, Sarwakai, Tangi Khaisara, Torwam.

for the regular army. The tribe of course cheerfully subscribed to these obligations and the new scheme of allowances was sanctioned with effect from 1 May 1895. The first distribution was made at Sheikh Budin in July of the same year.

Mr Bruce when appointed British Commissioner for the demarcation of the Durand Line had taken Mr L. W. King and Mr H. A. Anderson, the Deputy Commissioners of Dera Ismail Khan and Bannu, with him as his Political Assistants. As has been seen, events beyond the border dragged on to much greater length than had been anticipated. Consequently other arrangements became necessary and with the location of a military force at Wana, as a permanent measure, a Political Officer for South Waziristan was appointed with headquarters at Wana. Mr A. J. Grant, I.C.S., was the first incumbent. A similar post was about the same time created in the Tochi Valley of North Waziristan, the Daur inhabitants of which had petitioned to be taken under protection. Mr H. W. Gee, I.C.S., was the first Political Officer in the Tochi. This extension of protection to the Daurs of the Tochi had important effects on the adjoining Mahsud sections, chiefly the Jallal Khel (Bahlolzai). The Jallal Khel, whose happy hunting ground was the Tochi, had hitherto been able to indulge their raiding propensities unchecked in the Tochi and their trading ventures unmolested in Bannu. Now all this was changed. Government, though its arm was not long enough to reach them in their homes nor strong enough to give the Daurs very adequate protection was yet strong enough to nab them, all and sundry, when they came trading into Bannu. It was frontier custom no doubt, but an unpleasant innovation for the Jallal Khel. Trading lost its attraction. Raiding remained pretty much as it had been. So the Jallal Khel gave up trading. They sold off their pack animals and took to raiding both in the Tochi and in British India as their prime means of subsistence. Hence their previous comparative insignificance and subsequent importance.

Mulla Powinda found it convenient to withdraw from Mahsud country while the operations of 1894–5 were in progress. He turned up in Lower Daur in February 1895, but was chased out again by troops almost at once and was no more heard of till May, when he came to Kaniguram. The delimitation of the Durand Line, so far as Waziristan was concerned, was by that time complete, and his presence in Mahsud country was no

infringement of the latest tribal agreement with Government. He marked
the occasion of his return by addressing a letter to the Commissioner
asking to be included in any settlement made with the Mahsuds.
The Commissioner (Mr Bruce), as on a previous occasion, before the
attack on the camp at Wana, sent a verbal reply declining to hold any
communication with him except through the tribal maliks. Thus thrown
upon the maliks Mulla Powinda very soon discovered that he had very
little to fear from them. He started all the usual tricks—representing
himself as the agent and confidant of the Amir, raising 'shukrana' from
all whom he could intimidate into giving it, posing as *censor morum* and
interfering in a few easy cases, taking it on himself to speak for the tribe in
their dealings with Government officials and other tribes and maintaining
a bodyguard to convey his behests and carry out his decisions. By such
means he was rapidly able to consolidate his position, to cause a certain
amount of uneasiness to Government, and to arouse so much alarm and
despondency among the maliks that by July 1896, when the Mulla left
for Kabul, they petitioned for their whole country to be taken over by
Government as the only way of keeping him quiet. The Mulla entered
Afghanistan accompanied by 'a large party of the Dawar and Mahsud
Waziris, consisting of three hundred women and four hundred men and
including Saiyids, Ulamas, Maliks,[1] elders and ordinary tribesmen.' This
sanctimonious crew represented themselves as 'muhajirin' and asked the
Amir for land and maintenance in Afghanistan. They also asked for the
lands and houses which they had left in their own country to be sold
and the sale proceeds collected and sent after them. The Amir in his
dilemma consulted the Government of India, who replied that they had
no objection to the departure of those who preferred to live elsewhere
and that all who sent were at liberty to make their own arrangements
to dispose of their property in Waziristan. How much of this message
was passed on to the refugees does not appear, nor can it ever be known
what actually happened in Kabul during the Mulla's visit. The British
Agent reported that the Mulla was treated in very niggardly fashion,
and by September he was back again in Mahsud country. But no sooner
was he back than he was at his old tricks, hinting at an understanding
between the Amir and himself, writing to the local political authorities,

---

1. Note No. 11 at the end.

warning them to desist from the erection of fresh posts or other further encroachment in Waziristan, whether in Mahsud or Wazir country, and threatening them with hostile combinations, if his words fell unheeded. His words did fall unheeded, and all the world knows what happened next summer, when, beginning with the treacherous affair at Maizar in Madda Khel Wazir country, whither the Political Officer, Mr Gee and escort had gone to choose the site of a new post, one tribe after another rose against Government until the whole frontier, save only Mahsud country, was ablaze. Whether the Mulla instigated the Maizar attack or not is not proven, but he was intensely nervous all that summer, constantly[1] in communication with the local authorities, constantly demanding assurances or safe-conduct if he went here or there, constantly denouncing the forward policy of the time and as constantly protesting his innocence of all hostile intention. What advice he gave to his own tribesmen again is not known, but, if it was hostile, its weight was not sufficient to overcome their recollections of their recent lesson and the sight of military reinforcements at Jandola, Haidari Kach, and Sarwakai. So matters went on, Government and its officers regularly resolving to ignore the Mulla and as regularly finding themselves not altogether in a position to do so. By 1898 the Mulla's pretensions had so far advanced that we find him addressing his correspondence to the Lieutenant-Governor of the Punjab and no longer to local frontier officers. The Lieutenant-Governor replied to the Mulla's advances in the usual stereotyped formula, but he got more encouragement elsewhere. In July 1898 he received a letter from the Amir through Sardar Gul Muhammad Khan 'expressing regret that the Mulla returned from his last visit to Kabul with apparent feelings of dissatisfaction and assuring him that if he wished to go and see him, he was at liberty to do so'. This invitation however the Mulla did not for some time accept. His dilatoriness was not altogether inexplicable. It appears about this time to have occurred to Sir H. Barnes, then Foreign Secretary to the Government of India, that the policy of ignoring the Mulla was a mistake. A report was called for on the increase of his influence, which evoked a very interesting reply. The causes enumerated by Mr Watson, who had become Political Officer, Wana, in January 1899, were:

---

1. Note No. 12 at the end.

1. 'The chief of them is undoubtedly the countenance which the Mulla receives from the Amir or his agents,' with whom he was in constant correspondence;
2. 'his accumulation of arms and ammunition—believed to be privately supplied...from Afghanistan';
3. 'the encouragement which he gives to notorious badmashes.'

While enjoining on these and on his shaikhs' abstention from ordinary thieving and raiding, the Mulla here first appears as privily inciting to more glorious and daring deeds such as 'attacks on convoys or murders of European officers'. Mr Watson's report ends with the stolid declaration that he and all his subordinates consistently carried out Government's policy and ignored the Mulla. The answer that he got was that Government's policy was changed. Henceforth he was to try sailing upon the opposite tack and see whether he could not make a friend of the Mulla instead of an enemy and induce him to accept an allowance. This, it was anticipated, would pretty effectually draw his fangs. So it was that Mr Watson began to answer the Mulla's letters. In the autumn of 1899 the Lieutenant-Governor visited Mahsud country and at a jirga at Sarwakai, with His Honour's previous consent, the leading Mahsud maliks presented a petition on behalf of the Mulla asking Government 'having pardoned his past acts, to condescend to treat him with kindness, as becomes kings'. The petition was graciously received and the outcome of this regal condescension was apparent, when in the following February Mr Watson had a formal interview with the Mulla at Dotak[1] near Jandola. At this interview however the Mulla would not consent to receive an allowance and confined his conversation to matters of transient importance.

Within a few weeks of the Lieutenant-Governor's departure three serious offences were committed by Mahsuds. On the night of 15 December a gang of about twenty raiders waylaid a party of Border Military Police near Zarani Oba. Two sepoys were killed, three wounded, and five rifles taken. The same day four more Border Military Police sepoys were killed on convoy duty near Ngandi Oba on the road to Wana. Immediate barampta was made in Tank and the Bahlolzai jirga

---

1. The place where the Takki Zam and the Shahur stream meet.

was called in. While it was still in Tank, on 9 January another gang of forty men attacked Zam post, killed five of the occupants, and carried off four rifles and other loot. The mention of these affairs, though they were not allowed to interfere with Mr Watson's correspondence with the Mulla, compels a brief retrospect and an examination of the Mahsuds' current crime account. As usual, after the campaign of 1894–5, the Mahsuds were for some time comparatively well behaved, and for two years nothing more serious was recorded against them than an occasional looting of the mail between Jandola and Wana 'committed by certain men discontented with the distribution with a view to draw attention to their grievances'. Even during the troubled summer of 1897 the Mahsuds committed only one serious crime—the killing of two Bhitanni Levies. It was not thought politic to take this up at the time. In spite, or perhaps because, of this abstention, beyond some petty cattle lifting, nothing more happened until July 1898, when two more sepoys were killed on different occassions. In August Mr Anderson, who in 1896 had succeeded Mr Bruce as Commissioner of the Derajat, went on three months' leave and the Mahsud account was left to run on pending his return. In November various cases were taken up and settled by the method then in vogue. These resulted in a bill of damages amounting to Rs. 22,115.[1] But this was on account of 'offences committed in British territory and against British subjects and Government in protected areas' only. Besides these in what were called 'intertribal cases' there was a debit balance of Rs. 12,460 against the Mahsuds. According to Mr Anderson these intertribal cases were 'cases which occurred outside the limits of protected area in the hills and among tribesmen themselves'. Why these were taken up at all does not appear. During the year 1899, by hook or crook, recoveries amounting, in the first class of cases to Rs. 21,739 and in the second to Rs. 7,526 were effected, and had the sum above mentioned been the whole bill for the first and more important class of cases, all would have been well. But it was not the whole bill. Some old cases still remained to be taken up and further offences against Government and British subjects were committed during 1899. These resulted in a further bill of Rs. 18,466, so that, despite the recoveries, at the end of the

---

1. Of this sum no less than Rs. 7,260 were on account of raids—chiefly Jallal Khel raids—in the Tochi. The significance of this item will be noticed.

year, the Mahsuds were still nearly Rs. 20,000 down on cases other than intertribal cases. Among the tale of offences of 1899, which otherwise was not very serious, there now begin to loom large two forms of crime, both of which were more or less new to Mahsud annals. These were the ambushing of troops and other armed Government servants, with a view to securing their rifles, and attempts on the life of the Political Officer. Were these the outcome of the Mulla's private tuition? The local officers thought so, but could get no proof, and in the absence of proof they did not venture to propose any punishment but the enforcement of tribal responsibility by the infliction of a fine. Hence the bills of damages above-mentioned. For the serious offences of 1899 a further bill of Rs. 12,000 was prepared, making a total demand of approximately Rs. 30,000 to which had to be added another Rs. 9,000 'on account of the petty cases pending disposal'. What exactly these were, nobody but Mr Anderson seems to have understood at the time, or since. He however to his own satisfaction first declared 'the total charge' to be nearly Rs. 40,000 and later, after examining Mahsud assets, gave a revised bill of Rs. 35,000. The recovery even of the smaller sum he foresaw was going to be no very easy matter. Mr Anderson suggested two alternatives. The first alternative was a reversion to the rough and ready methods of Major Macaulay. The whole tribe could be put under blockade regardless of the effect on the well-disposed maliks and sections, regardless of the delicate negotiations recently opened with Mulla Powinda and of Mahsud recruitment for the South Waziristan Militia, the formation of which was then under consideration. The other alternative was a continuance of the methods employed with considerable success in the preceding year which may be described as the methods of Mr Bruce, with one important difference. Mr Bruce, as we have seen, on several occasions succeeded in getting the actual offenders surrendered to him. After his departure in 1896, except in one case[1] where the presence of his successor on tour enabled a very prompt and effective barampta to be made, this was no longer attempted. The methods employed to enforce reparation were first sectional barampta, where possible, and failing that, sectional negotiation and pressure on the maliks and jirgas of the sections concerned leading up to the ultimate invocation of the tribal responsibility of the three

1. Note No. 13 at the end.

Mahsuds. The recoveries of 1899 had put considerable strain on all this machinery and further recourse to these tactics, while offering small hope of speedy settlement, threatened to break down Mr Bruce's system altogether. The Punjab Government favoured blockade; the local officers were for carrying on the existing system. The real difficulty, as the local officers saw clearly enough, lay in the fact that, apart from the Mulla and his adherents, the tribe as a whole was behaving pretty well and many of the maliks responding with some degree of loyalty to the demands to which their position exposed them. These were naturally tired of being badgered to make good the delinquencies of persons who were not under their control and of whose protector, the Mulla, they were more and more mortally afraid. *Dale kasa, prang; dale kasa, kamar*. They were between the devil and the deep sea. And the devil seemed to be drawing nearer.

Clearly the position was one of considerable difficulty for all concerned. While it was being considered by the Government of India and the Punjab Government a local solution was found. Mr Anderson after four years' tenure of the Commissionership of the Derajat was about to go on long leave in the spring of 1900 and he wanted to bring about a settlement before he went. Early in March therefore he summoned the whole Mahsud jirga to Tank and frankly laid the bill (at the lower figure) before them. The assembled maliks promptly expressed their readiness to fall in with his wishes and concerted a scheme by which Rs. 20,000 could be produced at once. To raise this sum they gave up the tribal allowances for three months, half the pay of the levies for the same period, and the bulk of their share of the produce of the lands which the tribe still enjoyed in the Dera Ismail Khan District—a relic of Major Macaulay's original scheme for the opening of the Gumal Pass in 1878. They further offered to pay a tax on all Mahsud produce entering the Dera Ismail Khan and Bannu Districts and the Tochi, which it was hoped would realise Rs. 15,000 in six months. Mr Anderson accepted these arrangements, which appear to have been made in a genuine though perhaps unduly sanguine spirit of good will, and so in all love they parted. The settlement was approved by the Government of India, and Mr Merk succeeded Mr Anderson as Commissioner of the Derajat.

The new broom swept vigorously. Mr Merk discovered that owing to the confused system of keeping accounts the sum put down as due from the Mahsuds was Rs. 4,000 less than it ought to have been, and that the settlement only covered five out of the eight classes of offences in which the misdeeds of the Mahsuds were recorded. The classes omitted were the intertribal cases above-mentioned. For these an additional Rs. 17,000 was due. Mr Merk proposed to continue the tax on Mahsud produce until these excess sums had been collected. But these were not the only sums which required to be collected. During the spring and summer of 1900 further offences were committed.[1] Compared with more recent experiences they do not seem very terrible. In May the mail was looted in the Tiarza nullah near Wana, and a great pother was made about it. In June a levy sepoy was shot near Semi Kon tower in the Tochi.[2] In July an attack was made on a water picquet near Khajuri Kach, and all the time the tale of thieving and cattle lifting in the plains of the Derajat was steadily mounting. In the more serious offences the local officers still strongly suspected, though they could not prove, the complicity of Mulla Powinda. Meanwhile the Mulla, after being accorded the privilege of an interview with the Political Officer, had overcome the scruples which had kept him dumb on that interesting occasion, and intimated coyly that he was prepared to accept an allowance, provided that it were paid secretly. In token of good faith he at the same time declared his innocence in respect of the crimes of which he was suspected and protested his abhorrence of such sanguinary acts. His protestations were accepted very favourably and an allowance of Rs. 100 a month was sanctioned for him[3] 'though only with considerable hesitation; since it is a first class scoundrel that we are taking under our wing'. No Mahsud malik at this time was in receipt of an allowance of even half that sum and the Mulla's splendid stipend was thus a prodigality by no means, to be reconciled with the old policy. The recipient of such a stipend could no longer be snubbed, repressed, and ignored.

---

1. Note No. 14 at the end.
2. This tower no longer exists. It stood at the mouth of the nulla of the same name on the south bank of the Tochi river about half way between Miranshah and Boya.
3. The words are Lord Curzon's.

Chapter III

The year 1900 was pregnant with consequence. For some time past the Government of India had been growing more and more intolerant of the intervention of the Punjab Government between themselves and the officers on the spot, and more and more critical of the Punjab Government's methods and advice. In the spring of that year the new Viceroy, Lord Curzon, made a tour of the frontier. Amongst others who attended his progress was a young civilian named John Lorimer, who, after having made a great name for himself as Political Officer in the Tochi, had been caught up into the Secretariat. Mr Lorimer was the author of a significant phrase which found place in an official letter to the Punjab Government, issued almost immediately after Lord Curzon's arrival in Simla. 'With reference to the future management of the tribe', it runs, 'the Government of India will only observe that the best method of dealing with the Pathans of Waziristan appears to be still a matter for experiment'. Elsewhere Mr Lorimer explained his meaning more fully. He suggested that the lines on which Government was dealing with the Mahsuds were radically wrong and that Mr Bruce's maliki system, imported from Baluchistan, was not really suited to the democratic Wazir tribes. Mr Merk, though not the only begetter of this idea, seems to have been converted to it at the conference held by His Excellency at Dera Ismail Khan in April 1900, and thereafter did his best to foster it. In July he submitted to the Punjab Government a very able note in which he pointed out that not only were Baluchistan methods unsuited to Waziristan, but also that the main feature of the Sandeman system—*viz.*, penetration and occupation—had never been introduced, and that the whole attempt to secure control through the maliks had really broken down, when in 1894 nothing was done to those who killed the maliks by whom the murderers of Mr Kelly were handed up to justice. Mr Merk consequently proposed:

1. 'to make the allowances to the tribe instead of to selected maliks,

2. to deal with the tribe as a whole and to enforce tribal instead of individual responsibility in the case of offences'.

He also assessed the outstanding bill of damages against the Mahsuds at Rs. 60,000 and advocated the drastic remedy of placing the whole tribe under strict blockade, in the likely event of their failing to meet this liability at the autumn jirgas. The Punjab Government endorsed Mr Merk's views. He was summoned to Simla and there had the honour of further conference with His Excellency and the Lieutenant-Governor of the Punjab. Orders then issued sanctioning all his proposals. The Mahsud jirga was to be summoned and the demand made; if it were not met, the tribe was to be put under blockade and kept there till whatever fine had been announced should be recovered; further, the maliks were to be deposed and in future dealings were to be with the tribal or sectional jirga to whom the subsidy was to be paid; 'the practice of paying to selected individuals' it was added 'should cease, unless the jirga itself makes the selection and desires that the payment be so made'. The Mahsud allowances at the time amounted to Rs. 61,000 of which Rs. 28,000 were paid to the maliks and the balance through them to the Mahsud levies for border service. The levies were to be disbanded and the whole sum made available for distribution to the tribe. The pay of the 300 Mahsuds who were being recruited for the South Waziristan Militia was not to be taken into account. At the same time all Mahsuds settled on land in British India were to be turned out, as also were those who had enlisted in the South Waziristan Militia; both classes were to be reinstated when the blockade was over, provided that they had not participated in actual hostilities. With this many-chambered and fully loaded revolver in his pocket Mr Merk returned to Dera Ismail Khan.

On Mr Merk's return preparations were at once set in train. The 'great jirga of the Mahsuds' was summoned to Tank for 7 November. A Machiavellian invitation to a private interview was also, for somewhat murky reasons, sent[1] to Mulla Powinda; troops were warned to hold themselves in readiness; arms were procured for issue to border villages; special officers, amongst them Mr Lorimer, were named for blockade duty; funds were placed at the Commissioner's disposal and all other

---

1. But not accepted.

measures taken. While matters were thus in train, a Mahsud gang on the night of 23 October surprised the Border Military Police post at Kot Nasran, where only eight men out of the garrison of twelve were present, killed two of them and carried off ten Snider rifles and 1,200 rounds of ammunition. A military party turned out from Jandola to intercept the raiders. They effected contact at the junction of the Shuza and Khaisara nalas and knocked over one of the gang. But the officer commanding the party[1] was himself killed by this man, who, unable to flee with his fellows, hid in a depression and shot the officer down at short range. The great jirga of the Mahsuds duly came in on the date named, but in consequence of this affair and the alarm and suspicion thereby engendered, its number did not exceed five hundred. Mr Merk however accepted it as fully representative and got to business without delay. The maliks spoke first. They declared themselves helpless and repeated their request for the country to be taken over. This however, they admitted, was in direct opposition to the wishes of the tribe. Beyond that they had no suggestion to offer. Mr Merk then showed his hand and announced a fine of one lakh[2] of rupees. The maliks appeared 'relieved at the prospect of being extricated from a position which had become impossible'. On 9 November the jirga broke up. The tribal spokesmen promised every effort, but wished for time to consult the tribe and Mulla Powinda. They were given till 25 November and spent the interval in jirga at Kaniguram. But when the time ran out nothing had been decided and on 1 December the blockade began.

Mr Merk's blockade did not achieve so rapid a success as Major Macaulay's. At the end of five months only Rs. 4,000 had been recovered in cash, but rifles and revolvers assessed at Rs. 28,600 had been deposited and animals valued at Rs. 24,100 had been brought in. The Government of India then ordered that the balance of the fine must be paid in cash. Payments forthwith ceased. Mr Merk was driven to explain that 'Mahsud country is certainly self-supporting as a whole in respect of grain and livestock'—an admission that belied his earlier and more sanguine anticipations. Meanwhile the Mahsuds on their side had not

---

1. Lieutenant Hennessy.
2. The actual bill amounted to Rs. 1,87,000, but it was agreed that this could never be exacted and the reduced total was fixed at a good round sum.

been idle. They raided intermittently but vigorously in the Dera Ismail Khan and Bannu Districts, and in the Zhob Agency of Baluchistan, and they made numerous small attacks on the forces of Government, regular and irregular, forming the cordon round their country. In these they killed thirteen men, wounded ten, and carried off twenty-seven rifles. These exploits were followed by one even more serious. 'On the 6th August in broad daylight, the Militia post at Kashmir Kar[1] was attacked by a band of Mahsuds estimated to be 200 strong. The thirty men of the garrison were surprised, a Havildar, three sepoys, and three labourers were killed, the Native Officer commanding the post and three men were wounded, and thirty rifles, with a large quantity of ammunition and property were carried off.' In September and October there came a lull, 'the Mahsuds being occupied in fighting out a dispute of long standing with the Darwesh Khel' for possession of a rich area in the upper Baddar valley. In this, it may be remarked, they were completely successful, despite considerable activity in other directions, and Mahsud domination of upper Baddar dates from the Blockade year. On 23 September another longish pin was pushed well home. A gang of fifty Mahsuds led by a well-known outlaw named Nabi Bakhsh attacked a village near Sarai Naurang, twenty-five miles within the Bannu border. Attar Shah Singh, 'described as the headman of the village', his son and daughter, and four other persons were killed, and the gang got away with the loss of only four of its number, who however included two notorious badmashes Amar Din, Abdullai, and Khandar, a Tori Khel Wazir. On 2 November three sepoys of the 9th Bombay Infantry were killed in an ambuscade near Nili Kach and on the afternoon of the next day, about two miles from Khuzhma Khullah post a detachment of the 17th Bengal Infantry thirty-three strong, who were out for the protection of a survey party, was overwhelmed with a loss of twenty-three sepoys and six members of the survey party killed, five persons wounded, and the loss of about thirty rifles. This was more than a pin prick and provoked a prompt reaction. Government had for sometime been considering more active measures. Small columns, each about 1,000 strong with a Political Officer attached, were all ready at Datta Khel, Jandola, Sarwakai, and Wana. These were now directed to make incursions into Mahsud country and

---

1. On the borders of Sherani country, south of the Gumal river.

there destroy as many towers, take as many prisoners, drive off as many animals, and remove as much grain and fodder as they could. This first series of operations[1] began on 23 November and lasted for about five days. The tribes were completely taken by surprise and lost heavily in lives, prisoners, and property. Further operations followed and during the next two months Mahsud country was thoroughly harried. Makin was visited and partially destroyed, and the Khaisara, Shahur, Splitoi, Inzar, Shinkai, Shuza, and Shaktu valley were effectively penetrated. Mr Merk reckoned that the Mahsuds had suffered a loss of about two and a half lakhs in property and live stock, had had a hundred and thirty men killed, and about twice as many wounded. The casualties amongst the troops on the other hand were one British officer,[2] twenty-three other combatant ranks and three followers killed, and one hundred and ten of all classes wounded, of whom four were British officers. On 16 January 1902 the Mahsuds sent in a deputation of Saiyyids to tender submission and learn the terms. Negotiations lasted until 10 March, on which date the blockade was raised, though entire compliance in every particular had not been achieved. The terms were completion of the fine of one lakh, return of all[3] rifles taken and all cattle raided during the blockade, and the surrender of certain outlaws. During the negotiations, according to Mr Merk, the assembled jirga really did act with some show of authority. They appointed and despatched 200 chalweshtas to arrest the outlaws demanded, and though the arrests were not effected, the outlaws, Nabi Bakhsh included, were frightened away into Birmal and the tribe undertook never to let them back. In other respects the demands were complied with. The jirga gave promises of future good conduct and accepted responsibility for the behaviour of all Mahsuds including Mulla Powinda who took no part in the negotiations. So ended Mr Merk's blockade.

---

1. For details see the official account compiled under the orders of the Quartermaster General in India by Major G. B. Unwin—printed at Simla 1904.
2. Captain C. P. Down, Political Officer in the Tochi; he was shot after leading a rush on a tower in one of the Dodia Khel (Shabi Khel) villages on the Shaktu on 6 January 1902 and died the next day.
3. Seventy-one were demanded. The Mahsuds admitted having taken 65. They returned 41 of these and gave equivalent substitutes for the remainder.

In the month of November 1901 the districts and transborder tracts composing the North-West Frontier Province were separated from the Punjab and placed under the charge of a Chief Commissioner (Lieutenant-Colonel H. A. Deane). Colonel Deane was junior to Mr Merk, but Mr Merk consented to serve on and see his blockade through. When the blockade was raised the jirga was allowed to disperse for the *Id* with orders to re-assemble at Tank on 24 March. On 29 March the Chief Commissioner interviewed them, accepted their formal submission and assurances,[1] and announced the restoration of the tribal allowances at the figure (Rs. 61,000 per annum) recommended by Mr Merk. Of this sum, Rs. 54,000 was for equal distribution, after mutual accounts had been adjusted, between the three main branches Alizai, Bahlolzai, and Shaman Khel. The balance was reserved for allocation at the discretion of the Political Agent to prominent supporters of Government—in fact to those among the old maliks who did something for it. The distribution of the main sum between the three main sections was worked out with extraordinary minuteness. This, Mr Merk said, was done at the wish of the tribe, and he added 'So far as I am able to judge, the Mahsuds have not the slightest intention of permitting anyone to do what may lead to the forfeiture of the tribal allowances and to the rescission of the present settlement.... If nothing unforseen occurs, I see no reason why the settlement should not work. There will be difficulties of course...but one may reasonably hope that they will be overcome and that affairs will go smoothly till they become matters of routine.'

Mr Merk's revolutionary proposals had been endorsed by Colonel Deane and accepted without demur by the Government of India. But it was not long before it became apparent that his hopes were unreasonable. Within three months of Mr Merk's departure we find Mr Johnston, Political Officer at Wana, reporting that the new scheme was unworkable. In the first instance, he said, Mr Merk, though he did not report the fact, had laid it down that the fine was to be paid in exactly the same proportions as the allowances were to be distributed and had laid the charge of adjusting accounts—an impossible task—on the Political Agent. Again, most of the old maliks and practically the whole of the large class whom he called mu'tabars had held aloof from the settlement. Further,

---

1. Note No. 15 at the end.

the sum reserved for deserving maliks was wholly inadequate, and finally, dealing with the Mahsuds through Mr Merk's 'great jirga of the Mahsuds' a disorderly mob always over 1,500 strong, was as impracticable as it was expensive. Mr Johnston therefore asked for an additional Rs. 9,000 per annum, thus raising the total allowances to Rs. 70,000 per annum. Of this Rs. 54,000, as arranged by Mr Merk, was to be 'tumani', for the tribe as a whole, and the balance Rs. 16,000 was to be 'maliki' for the old maliks and mu'tabars, who however were 'to enter the tuman as vakils appointed by the tuman'. Their salaries were to follow the recognised tribal shares, but only those who could get themselves recognised as vakils by the tuman were to draw pay and any vakil who did not work was to get nothing. Once again Colonel Deane endorsed the proposal and the Government of India, though Lord Curzon poured out the vials of his sarcasm on this 'conglomerate scheme' and the vacillation out of which it arose, found themselves compelled to accept it. But they did so without conviction. 'No patchwork scheme—and all our present recent schemes', said Lord Curzon, 'blockade, allowances, etc., are mere patchwork—will settle the Waziristan problem. Not until the military steam-roller has passed over the country from end to end, will there be peace. But I do not want to be the person to start that machine.'

Chapter IV

Mulla Powinda had been in correspondence with Mr Merk at intervals all through the blockade period. But he did not attend the March jirgas nor take any part in Mr Merk's settlement. To give the Mahsuds time to redeem the various pledges which had been accepted from them for full compliance with orders—chiefly those for the return of stolen cattle—the Government of India had ordered that the newly sanctioned allowances should not be paid out before January 1903. And in the intervening period, as has been shown, an increment of Rs. 9,000 and a new scheme of distribution had been proposed and approved. So it came about that Mr Merk's settlement, which he had heralded with such a fanfare, was scrapped before it had been put in practice at all. What followed cannot be better told than in Mr Johnston's own words.[1] 'This fortnight has been entirely taken up with a Mahsud jirga. The jirga was fully representative, including the Mulla Powinda and every other man of importance in the tribe, and numbered about 3,500. The tribe unanimously agreed to do away with all the tribal representatives given last year, who were men of small account, and to include in these representatives all the old maliks and other representative men, who at the last distribution had stood aloof in the hopes of obtaining separate recognition. The work of selection of these is now progressing'.

Early in April 1902 while the Mahsud jirga, which had met in Tank after the blockade was still sitting, had occurred the incident referred to in the records of the time as the Toi Khulla outrage. This was an unprovoked attack on a small party of the 27th Punjabis moving between Toi Khulla and Kajuri Kach in which eight sepoys were killed and eight rifles taken. The Mahsuds declared this offence, like the Khuzhma Khulla affair of the previous year, to be the work of the outlaws recently driven into Birmal and living there under the protection of the Afghan Governor, for whose actions under the terms of their agreement the tribe could not

---

1. South Waziristan Diary for fortnight ending on 14 February 1903.

116

be held responsible. This is the first mention that we have of Mahsud outlaws living in Afghanistan and interfering to disturb the relations of Government with the tribe, and in the light of subsequent events it is significant. The case itself was settled in a fairly satisfactory manner. Further enquiries had shown that the gang, which was led by Mianji and Barak, Abdur Rahman Khel, and Ashiq, Palli Khel, had been harboured in Mahsud country before committing the offence and, as usual, suspicion had arisen that the offence was committed at the instigation of Mulla Powinda. The tribe was ordered to bring him in for trial. This they did. He was tried (perhaps only a *pro forma* trial) at Sarwakai and acquitted. The outlaws were then expelled from Birmal by the orders of the Amir and arrived in Mahsud country. Ashiq was surrendered, tried, and convicted. Mianji himself was brought to within four miles of Sarwakai, when he made good his escape and Guldad, one of the maliks, his captors, was killed in the resultant squabble. Mahsud country was too hot to hold Mianji and he fled to Kabul. Barak was killed soon after in a petty tribal affray. For their complicity in the offence the Mahsuds were fined Rs. 6,700, which was promptly recovered. Apart from this and from an affair of sheep-stealing near Narai Oba on the borders of the Wana protected area the Mahsuds gave no serious trouble, and, as already mentioned, their new allowances on an enhanced scale, of which according to Mr Johnston 'the definition and distribution was left entirely to the tribe', were paid in February 1903.

How far such a statement can ever be wholly accurate is a matter on which some scepticism may be pardonable. But the new distribution however affected certainly seems to have been successful, and the summer of 1903, during which Captain Bowring succeeded Mr Johnston as Political Agent, passed without any act of hostility against Government on the part of those, and there must inevitably have been some, who were disappointed by it. The limits of the protected area in South Waziristan were at the same time clearly defined. In the Tochi this was not attempted, but the Jallal Khel who showed a disposition to revive their old habits of raiding there, were repressed by the remainder of the tribe.

It was during this year (1903) that Lord Kitchener made his trip from Wana to Datta Khel through Shawal, and that the Anglo-Afghan

Commission passed down the Durand Line settling cases between the tribes on either side of the line, from the Kurram to the Gumal.

The records of the time give great prominence to the bickerings of the Mahsuds among themselves and even more to their squabbles with their Bhitanni and Tori Khel Wazir neighbours, in the settlement of which Mulla Powinda tried without marked success to play a leading role. But so far as Government were concerned the Mahsuds behaved well. There were only three cases pending against them at the autumn jirga and before the close of the year Mulla Powinda who seems in this, as in the attempted adjudication of intertribal disputes, to have been seeking a super-tribal position, actually apprehended and sent in to Sarwakai 'accompanied by forty Tumani Vakils' an Urmur offender who had been sentenced to three years imprisonment and had escaped from custody. Tribal opinion of course would not be nearly so strong over the surrender of an Urmur as of a Mahsud, but even so it was a remarkable performance.

Mention has already been made of the recruitment of Mahsuds in the Indian Army and in the South Waziristan Militia. The former idea had been in the air for a long time and the 124th Baluchistan Infantry had actually had one company of them (old style, a hundred and fourteen strong) since 1898. After the blockade in 1903 the 130th raised a similar company. This was the extent of Mahsud recruitment in the Indian Army till 1911.

The Waziristan Militias were a new venture, another of the new ideas launched in or about the year 1900, as the outcome of the application of Lord Curzon's vigorous mind to frontier problems, after the mess of 1897 had been swept up. The intention, which was part of a general policy, was to create in Waziristan two forces, with headquarters respectively at Wana and at Miranshah, of a higher standard of discipline and training than the old levies, where such existed, to incorporate in them such elements from existing forces as were capable of absorption and with the force thus created, equipped, and armed (with M.H. rifles) by Government, and 'composed, in equal moieties of local tribesmen and of recruits from outside sources, who were for the most part, to be British subjects',[1] to take over from the regular army the burden of occupying and policing those portions of tribal territory of which the occupation

---

1. Government of India despatch No. 179 of 1904.

and policing were considered necessary. The sepoy's pay was fixed at Rs. 10 per mensem without rations and that basic rate was sufficient to attract recruits in plenty. The Mahsuds, the most important tribe in Waziristan, were naturally drawn upon. Three companies, each about 100 strong, were recruited from them in the South Waziristan Militia, one from each of their main tribal divisions, and one similar company in the North Waziristan Militia. Enlistment amongst the mounted infantry of the two corps brought the total recruitment of Mahsuds up to nearly four hundred in the South Waziristan Militia and about one hundred and twenty in the Tochi Corps. The progress of the two Militias was naturally retarded by the Mahsud blockade, but the portion of them that remained intact took a prominent part in the active operations which marked its final phase. On its conclusion both corps were enlarged and re-organised and made rapid progress. During the years 1903 and 1904, besides furnishing an escort for the British representative on the Anglo-Afghan Commission, Mr J. S. Donald, for various survey parties and for the engineers in charge of the Gumal road to Wana which had been sanctioned, the Militias took over one after another all the posts in Waziristan which had been formerly held by regulars, except Jandola. This was indeed setting the poacher to act as gamekeeper. But the officers selected to command the new Militias (Lieutenant-Colonel Harman and Captain Ferguson-Davie) and their assistants were men eminently suited for their task, and they achieved a measure of success which was in reality deceptive. By the admission of Lord Curzon himself it was greater than any of the warmest friends of the Militia scheme had anticipated. The future was therefore contemplated with a confidence which the boldness of the venture and the excessive speed at which it had been pushed on really in no way justified. The crash was not very long in coming. In September 1904 at Sarwakai an Abdur Rahman Khel sepoy of the South Waziristan Militia murdered Captain Bowring, the Political Agent, by night as he lay asleep on the roof of the post. The murderer was overpowered and executed, but signs were not lacking that his crime, for which no proximate cause could be ascribed, had the approbation of some at least among his fellows. As usual Mulla Powinda was suspected to be at the bottom of the affair, but proof, again as usual, was not at the time forthcoming.

In the following February Colonel Harman, Commandant of the
South Waziristan Militia, was murdered at Wana by another Mahsud
sepoy, this time an Astonai Shabi Khel. The officiating Political Agent
(Mr Howell, I.C.S.*) found that the murder was the outcome of a
Mahsud conspiracy in the ranks, the object of which was to murder
all the British officers at Wana, and to seize the fort at Wana and all
its contents and hand them over to Mulla Powinda, who, it must be
remembered, openly called himself King of Waziristan. The Political
Agent, with less than one month's experience of the Agency, accordingly
found himself compelled, suddenly and in the dead of night, to set
about disarming and cast forth the Mahsud element in the corps, which
amounted to nearly one-quarter of its total strength. The task was one of
some difficulty, but it was completed within twenty-four hours without
untoward incident. The Government of India were naturally much put
out at the setback to their policy thereby involved and were disposed to
query the necessity for the action taken. When the Chief Commissioner's
final report reached them however they somewhat grudgingly conceded
that the situation justified all that had been done, but complained, not
without cause, that the facts of the situation in Waziristan had not been
properly reported to them by the local administration. The evidence
upon the record of these events is enough to satisfy any reasonable man
of the reality of the conspiracy above-mentioned and, as was afterwards
proved to the satisfaction of the Government of India, such a conspiracy
could scarcely have existed without the support or at any rate the
connivance of Mulla Powinda. But once more, at the time, no definite
proof was forthcoming. It is indeed only by a stroke of luck that in such
circumstances definite proof ever can be forthcoming. In the absence
of proof, since the Mahsud tribe as a whole continued to behave well,
Government preferred to draw no inferences and to avoid a breach with
the Mulla. Mr Howell was replaced as Political Agent by Mr Crump,
I.C.S., for whom indeed he had originally only been stopping the gap,
and the new Political Agent, backed by a new Commandant, set about
the enlistment of fresh Mahsuds for the local Militia under a new system
of tribal guarantees. The Mahsud company in North Waziristan, being

---

* ὃς καὶ ταῦτα ξυνέγραψεν (The writer of these pages)

very much in the minority and at some distance from their homes, were not exposed to quite the same temptations as their fellows in the other corps and, though shaken by these events and by the wave of fanaticism which swept through Waziristan in 1905, were kept in hand.

Chapter V

Consideration of these events in the South Waziristan Militia has led us away from the main theme. It is now time to hark back. The phase which opens with the end of the blockade and the inauguration of the Frontier Province is marked by several features new to Mahsud history. These are the dominant role played by Mulla Powinda as leader of the tuman; his recognition by Government and subsequent fall from grace; his struggle with the old maliks; the depredations of Mahsud outlaws residing in Afghan territory and their connection with the Mulla, and the campaign of murderous outrages and attempts, responsibility for which was finally laid at the Mulla's door. With it all the tribe as a whole continued to behave pretty well, but, owing to the factors of disturbance above mentioned, crises more or less serious were not infrequent. The first of these occurred in July 1904 when the outlaws, who had once more secured a refuge in Afghan territory, led by the notorious Mianji and Ahmad Khan, attacked Khuni Burj post in the Zhob Agency, killed the Jemadar in Command and one sepoy, wounded another, and carried off all the arms and ammunition in the post. The tribe was exonerated from complicity in this affair. Protest was made at Kabul and the Amir threatened Mianji and his gang, to whom lands had been given at Ghozba near Ghazni, with deportation to Afghan Turkistan. Nothing however came of this, if indeed it was ever meant seriously, and the affair blew over.

In June 1905 *ex*-Jemadar Kastor of the South Waziristan Militia and two of his brothers, Abdur Rahman Khel, who were closely related to Captain Bowring's murderer, were shot by Afridis of the Militia near Sarwakai in circumstances which suggest that the Afridis may have laid a plot for them. Bad blood undoubtedly existed between the Afridis of the Militia, especially Subedar Mohibullah who was in command on this occasion, and the Mahsuds, especially the Mahsud *ex*-Militiamen. Another Abdur Rahman Khel named Muhabbat, son of the notorious malik, Jambil, who was one of the murderers of Mr Kelly in 1893, was wounded and taken prisoner in the same affair. The view officially taken was that Subedar Mohibullah's action was justifiable and praiseworthy and he was rewarded for it. But whether justifiable or not it caused considerable resentment among the Mahsuds and before the affair could be settled, Jambil himself was arrested inside the post at Sarwakai and a carbine was produced which he was charged with having concealed about his person. He was tried and convicted of having entered the post with intent to murder the Naib Tahsildar and sentenced to ten years imprisonment. In this case Mulla Powinda sent in previous warning of Jambil's intentions, but with what motive he did so much remains uncertain. He was at the time at the height of his struggle with the old maliks, whose discontent with the settlement of 1903 and their resultant position was steadily growing, and had every reason for desiring the removal of one of the most forceful personalities from the other side. Throughout the summer of 1905 Mulla Powinda made repeated attempts to settle the long standing quarrel between the Mahsuds and the Utmanzai Wazirs of the Tochi, especially the Tori Khel, but with no permanent results except to consolidate his position as the dominant factor in Mahsud politics. The tribe as a whole continued to behave well in spite of the fact that work on the Gumal road, which was finished this year, was given to outsiders—the Mahsud rates being considered exorbitant—and that work on the Paharpur canal, which was promised to them, did not begin. But in November 1905 their record was again stained by another murder of a British officer. This time the victim was Captain Donaldson, R.F.A., Brigade Major at Bannu, who was shot from behind a culvert just outside the cantonment. His assailant was a Shabi Khel Mahsud, an *ex*-Militiaman and one of a gang who went out to seek revenge for the imprisonment of seven men found guilty of complicity in Colonel Harman's murder. The prosecution of this case for a time suspended relations with the Mahsuds, but ultimately it was settled. Three members of the gang were first surrendered by Mulla Powinda. This roused a spirit of emulation among the old maliks, the Mulla's opponents, and a fourth man Umar Khan was brought in by Mehr Dil,[1] Mal Khel. The fifth man, Pashakai, who was related to the Mulla, was strong enough to defy both parties and remained at large. His house was

---

1. See Appendix II.

burnt and his crops destroyed by a tribal lashkar and Rs. 10,000 were forfeited from the tribal allowances in lieu of his surrender.

Throughout the correspondence dealing with this affair Mr Crump did not cease to reiterate his belief, and to state his reasons for holding it, that the Mulla was at the bottom of all the trouble. The Chief Commissioner accepted this view, but the Government of India, while approving the recommendations of the local officers, did not commit themselves to any expression of opinion as to the Mulla's guilt. Even so, it is somewhat startling to learn that about this time, with the approval of the Government of India, the Mulla was given a grant of land in British India. This grant was publicly announced at the autumn jirga. The list of recipients of maliki allowances, *i.e.* Rs. 16,000 per annum out of the total allotment of Rs. 70,000 was at the same time revised by a committee appointed at the request of the tribal jirga. It consisted only of the Political Tahsildar and Mulla Powinda, and their proposals were then submitted to the section concerned and approved by them in consultation with the Political Agent. The effect of this revision was to reduce the number of maliks from a figure in the neighbourhood of 1,500 to one near 300. The avowed object of the first move was 'to bind the Mulla by ties of personal interest to Government and incidentally to reduce his paramount influence'; of the second, to give the tribe alternative leaders and 'to strengthen the oligarchy of really efficient maliks'.

If the reader of this monograph will exercise a little careful reflection on these proposals, on the inevitable effect on the rest of any one which might be successful and on the means adopted to carry them out, the writer will be spared the necessity of comment. But that the grant of land should have been made at this jirga is all the more surprising, because at it the jirga, in response to the Mulla's intrigues, declared that the tribe could no longer be responsible for Mahsuds in the Militia. The Mahsud element in the South Waziristan Militia was consequently once again disbanded. The Mahsud company in the North Waziristan Militia remained however unaffected and continued to do good service. A week or two after the jirga the Mulla set out for Kabul with a following of sixty men. About the same time Jaggar,[1] Abdur Rahman Khel, the famous raider who led the Mahsud swordsmen in their attack on the camp at Wana in 1894, with

---

1. Note No. 16 at the end.

a bunch of his fellow tribesmen also went off to join Mianji at Ghozba near Ghazni. But the two parties went separately. The Mulla's reception in Kabul is said to have been cool. But the coolness must have been speedily overcome. For he received a cash present of several thousand rupees and by the middle of December he was back again in Mahsud country. We are told that the acceptance of the grant of land did seriously affect the Mulla's position and several attempts upon his life by his tribal opponents which occurred about this time are connected with the diminution of his prestige thus caused. They are at least equally likely to have been the work of some of the 1,200 men who owed the loss of their maliki to the Mulla and there is little sign in the record of current events of any real curtailment of the Mulla's power. He was at any rate not long in getting it back and was soon well able to continue his struggle with the maliks 'a struggle fraught with menace to the peace of the border'. No serious crime was indeed actually committed, but reports of the despatch to various destinations of murderous emissaries, several of whom were arrested, maintained an intolerable state of tension. The Political Agent (Mr Crump) now prepared a dossier against the Mulla which 'satisfied the Government of India that the allegations against him' in connection with the three recent murders of British officers and some at least of the numerous subsequent alarms of the same nature 'were well founded'. The grant of land and the special secret allowance of Rs. 100 a month were accordingly withdrawn under the orders of the Government of India, a formal warning was given to the tribe of their responsibility for the acts of every member of the tribe, and their allowances were suspended until such time as they should give proof of a desire for friendly relations.

About the same time (August 1907) a Wazir Mulla from Khost named Lala Pir, who represented himself as sent by the Amir, arrived in Waziristan and after touring the country reached Razmak, where a joint Wazir-Mahsud jirga was held and excitement rose to a high pitch. From the jirga, so we read, a lashkar of Mahsuds of all sections went off and raided the cattle of the Narmi and Bakka Khel Wazirs of the Bannu District. This, in the absence of special reason, of which there is no trace upon the record, seems a curious direction for anti-Government fervour to take, but the raid was certainly committed in British India, and may have been a deliberate gesture of defiance. Two more emissaries of murder were at the same time despatched by the Mulla, one to Wana and one to the Tochi. Both were arrested. The Wana man made a full confession that he had been sent to kill the Political Agent, but Government, though admitting that the warning given had been defied, did not think proper to do more than order the tribal allowances of the Mahsuds to be withheld and the Mulla (once again) to be ignored in all future dealings with the tribe.

It is noteworthy that in their despatch reviewing the situation the Government of India first proclaimed their conviction 'that the first step towards the settlement of the Mahsud country is the opening up of a good road from the Tochi to Wana'. They owed the idea to Mani Khan, Sperkai, who had presented a petition to this effect about this time to the Chief Commissioner. The tribal jirga was summoned to hear these terms. Only the maliks and their adherents attended and they said that 'they could do nothing to control the Mulla', who meanwhile (November 1907) repaired once more to Kabul. He returned with a present of Rs. 7,000 and 2,000 cartridges and a replenished stock of windy promises, and assumed a defiant attitude. 'From this time onward' we are told, 'political work was at a standstill, raiding by the Mulla's Shaikhs, the Mahsud outlaws and the Abdur Rahman Khel grew[1] lively' and the despatch of fanatical emissaries went on intermittently. On 13 March 1908 the Mahsud outlaws brought matters to a head. They had been exhorted by the Mulla to kill the Political Agent and the Political Tahsildar and on being informed that these two would travel from Sarwakai to Murtaza on that day, they laid an ambush in the Khuzhma Nulla. The information was erroneous, but the raiders met the Political Agent's bearer and the Political Tahsildar's munshi travelling under badragga escort and killed them both, mutilating the bearer's body. The property they for the most part left untouched. The Political Agent ordered an immediate barampta of all the Mahsuds upon whom he could lay hands. Three hundred and seventy-nine men and one thousand eight hundred and eighty-four head of cattle were seized and

---

1. Mianji and his followers had been increasingly active since the affair of Khuni Burj in July 1904. In 1905 they attacked two posts of the Levy Corps in Zhob; in October 1906 they murdered two sowars of the same corps on the Zhob road and in 1907 besides various offences in Zhob and Sherani country they committed five offences in or on the borders of Waziristan of which the worst was the murder of a sepoy and a dhobi at Spinkai Kach in May.

the tribal jirga, without Mulla Powinda, was ordered to Tank to meet the Chief Commissioner (Sir Harold Deane). The jirga was told that the allowances then due would be withheld and those for the year 1908–9 set aside to compensate sufferers from Mahsud lawlessness. They were also clearly warned that further misbehaviour would lead the whole tribe into serious trouble. Sir Harold Deane however could find no means of arriving at a working arrangement and was forced to the conclusion that war was the only remedy. The jirga had consisted mainly of the maliks and their followers. Mulla Powinda at once held a counter jirga of the tuman at Kaniguram and urged his hearers not to come to any settlement with Government except through him. He enlisted a bodyguard of a hundred well armed men and sent a deputation of another hundred to Kabul to ask assistance. These indeed were turned back at Urgun, but this did not stop the constant passage to and fro of single envoys and the spreading of the usual rumours. The Political Agent had another abortive jirga at Sarwakai in May. But before the next act in the drama there was a sudden and complete change of cast amongst the protagonists on the Government side. Sir Harold Deane collapsed and after a short illness died on his way home to England. He was replaced as Chief Commissioner by Sir George Roos-Keppel who at once caused the post of Resident in Waziristan to be created and filled it with Mr J. S. Donald, an officer with great experience of Waziristan. Mr Crump at the same time went on leave and Captain R. A. Lyall became Political Agent in his stead. Immediately on his appointment Mr Donald saw a Mahsud jirga at Sarwakai. It consisted of about six hundred men, chiefly maliks. It was agreed, after they had put forward various requests, that they should go off and discuss the situation with their sections and when they had done so, should meet the Resident again and hold a proper jirga. The maliks called a tribal jirga to Kaniguram. The Mulla held a rival meeting at Karamma and led a following 3,000 strong to Barwand, six miles north of Sarwakai. There the gathering dispersed for lack of supplies. The Resident was accordingly able to hold his big jirga at Sarwakai in August and handled it with skill. The upshot of the meeting, at which about 4,000 Mahsuds were present, was that the tribe promised good behaviour and the Resident promised to pay the tribal allowances due in October, if reparation were made meanwhile for outstanding offences.

These included a dacoity at Saggu in the Dera Ismail Khan District in which property valued at nearly half a lakh of rupees was looted; an attack on a Border Military Patrol near Girni, in which the Jemadar in command, one Havildar, and ten sepoys were killed, one sepoy wounded and fourteen rifles were carried off; and an attack on the Tiarza tower, near Wana, in which two sepoys were killed, two wounded, and two rifles taken. In all these affairs the leading part had been taken by Mianji, Abdur Rahman Khel and his gang from Afghanistan. At Tiarza however fortune was on the side of the Militia. They gave rather better than they got, killing three and wounding two of their assailants, and amongst the slain was Mianji himself, whose death was thought worthy of a press communique by the Government of India. His removal materially eased the situation. In December the Chief Commissioner saw a small jirga of Mahsud maliks at Tank and ordered them to hand in sixty good breech-loading rifles as security for the future good behaviour of the tribe. By January the rifles had been handed in and the maliks, backed by the Resident, had made considerable headway in detaching the tuman from the Mulla. In March was held an enormous jirga at Tank, at which over 7,000 Mahsuds were present. At this meeting the allowances for the second half of the year (1908–9) were paid, numerous outstanding cases were settled, and the deposited rifles were allowed to be redeemed at Rs. 250 each. With the sum thus realised Rs. 15,000 compensation for the Saggu and Girni offences was paid and according to the Political Agent (Captain Patterson who relieved Captain Lyall in December 1908) 'the year[1] closed with peace and goodwill'.

The Chief Commissioner was less optimistic. Indeed he had cause for misgiving. Sir George Roos-Keppel's first review of border administration is a noteworthy document and repays study. In it he lays stress upon three factors all adverse and all, in the magnitude which they now assumed, new. The first and most important of these was the malign influence of Afghan intrigue, an old evil in a new guise. This Sir George, quoting and confirming the opinion of his predecessor, had no hesitation in ascribing to the deliberate policy of the Amir. Whether that charge is capable of proof or not, it is perhaps significant that the new shape which the trouble took was everywhere uniform. The Afghan governors of all the

1. *i.e.* the administrative year April 1908–March 1909.

eastern districts, he says, afforded an asylum and maintenance to gangs of criminals, refugees from tribal territory, and outlaws from British India, and encouraged them to raid across the Durand Line. The second adverse development was the dimensions to which the practice of kidnapping, especially of Hindus, had grown. It formed indeed the recurrent motif of all raiding at this time. The third was the great extension and improvement of tribal armaments by the purchase and importation from the Persian Gulf of modern rifles in large numbers. All these developments had affected the Mahsuds and Sir George mentions as an established fact that Mulla Powinda had also received a grant of lands in Afghanistan. But after the removal of Mianji none of the new troubles had in Mahsud country the same prominence as they had elsewhere, or as they might easily attain with such a nucleus as the Mulla and his shaikhs and such material as the Mahsud tribe for it to impregnate. These developments obviously favoured the Mulla's schemes, but he was none the less now in a more difficult position than he had been for years. Government's reversion to the policy of ignoring him, which has been described as a belated attack of sanity, lost nothing from the vigour with which Mr Donald applied it, and in his opening round with the Mulla the new Resident had scored heavily on points. The maliks too, backed by him, showed signs of greater cohesion amongst themselves and consequently of a stronger hold over the tribe. The Mulla while losing ground with the tribe was definitely in opposition to Government. His adherents and some of his relatives were known to have taken a leading part in the Saggu raid and other offences. Mianji, whom, if he had known more of Islamic history, he might have dubbed Saif-ul-Haqq, like a second Khalid, was gone, and his hopes, either of acceptance by the tribes or recognition by Government as the ruler of Waziristan, seemed to be fading away. Drastic action alone could restore the position, but his first move was a clumsy one. May be it was forced upon him by unruly followers whom he could not control, or, as seems more probable, it was a *coup manque*, having been originally intended for an attack on the post. It consisted in an attack (April 1909) by a very large gang of Mahsuds on the Bhitanni Village of Khecha in the protected area near Jandola. Two or three Bhitannis were killed or wounded and some rifles carried off. A heavy fire was later opened on Jandola post, but without effect. The maliks at once came in, disclaimed all part in this affair and gave a guarantee of forty-eight rifles for its settlement. At the same time, so curious are the workings of the tribal mind, they petitioned for the restoration of the Mulla's allowances, a request which was promptly refused. It will be remembered that under Mr Johnston's settlement of 1903 the Mahsud allowances had been raised to Rs. 70,000 per annum, of which Rs. 54,000 were paid to the tuman and Rs. 16,000 to the maliks. The Mulla now undertook to procure a redistribution among the tuman of the maliks' share. The maliks countered by offering to surrender their share and a confused period of tortuous negotiation followed. In August the Mulla paid a flying visit to Kabul and on his return made overtures to the Resident and for a time stopped the raiding. Recognition however did not follow and the raiding began again. Numerous serious offences were committed and all had this feature in common that each one was the work of a large gang of Mahsuds. These culminated in the affair of 11 March 1910 at Banda Ayyaz Khan near Lakki in the Bannu District in which something like a pitched battle was fought between the Border Military Police, troops, and a gang of thirty-two Mahsuds. Captain Stirling, D.S.O., and six sepoys were killed and twelve men wounded on the side of Government. Of the raiders eight men, including the notorious Kamil, Shabi Khel, Shaikh of the Mulla and the leader of the gang, were killed and three wounded and taken prisoner. These were afterwards hanged. It is interesting to note in the correspondence of this period that Waziristan was then costing Government Rs. 18 lakhs a year apart from military expenditure, that Sir G. Roos-Keppel, in spite of the improvement in the situation brought about by Mr Donald, thought that there was no ultimate alternative between evacuation and the extension of administrative control, and only favoured the latter because he feared the first to be impossible; and finally that about this time proposals were tentatively made for a substantial recruitment of Mahsud levies, *i.e.* the khassadars of the future—a scheme which Sir George described as 'thinly disguised black-mail'. The expediency of giving grants of land in British India to the Mahsuds and other transborder tribes was also discussed, but inconclusively, and the extension of recruitment amongst Mahsuds for the Indian Army. Mr Crump also caused a considerable flutter by a note which he wrote while at home on leave (1908–9) advocating a policy of internal control of Mahsud country based upon the military occupation of Razmak and the construction of a road from Thal to Wana—in short a pretty accurate adumbration of the policy subsequently adopted. But the contrast between Mr Crump's estimate of expenditure and the actuals of later date is startling. Mr Crump allowed Rs. 15 lakhs for initial expenditure on roads and posts, and Rs. 14 lakhs for annual recurring political and civil expenditure.[1] Meanwhile with the consent of the maliks, the tribal allowances, amounting on each occasion to Rs. 35,000, were drawn in September and March and paid away to various sufferers from Mahsud depredations. The bill however continued to mount and in May 1910 a serious dacoity took place at Kot Sultan in the Dera Ismail Khan District in which four Hindus were kidnapped and held to ransom by Mahsud marauders of minor sections. Sectional barampta followed and procured the release of the prisoners. Raiding however did not cease and in June another serious dacoity took place at Vihoa in the Dera Ghazi Khan District of the Punjab, also the work of petty sections. Again, fortune favouring, sectional barampta was employed with such effect that the ringleaders were handed up for trial and the property returned in full. This example set the ball rolling, the notorious Abdur Rahman Khel being the first to show the way. In the reports of the time this almost miraculous conversion is ascribed chiefly to the personal influence of the new Political Tahsildar over Muhammad Jan, the leading Abdur Rahman Khel raider, on whom Mianji's mantle had fallen. But in the Agency other and more sinister influences were and are generally believed to have been at work, and much of the trouble of after years with this section is ascribed to an arrangement alleged to have been made *sub rosa* somewhere about this time, whereby the Abdur Rahman Khel should receive a series of underhand payments which exactly doubled their tribal share of the sanctioned allowances. Anyhow, section after section came in, even the Shabi Khel, with the son and nephew of Mulla Powinda, who were themselves maliks, at their head, and by the autumn almost all cases against the Mahsud tribe had been settled. In the course of the jirgas by which these results were achieved the tribe represented, with singular unanimity, that the main root of all the trouble was the dissatisfaction

---

1. Waziristan under existing arrangements costs about Rs. 60 lakhs a year, civil expenditure only.

felt throughout Mahsud country at the present form of distribution of the maliki allowances. The implied request for a redistribution was favourably received and the further petition for increased enlistment in the army was also accepted. Orders were very speedily given that each of three regiments (the 127th, 129th, and 130th Baluchis) should have three old style companies of Mahsuds in addition to the single company already enlisted in the 124th. Recruitment for these began at once and proceeded satisfactorily. The final request of the jirgas was, once again, for the restoration of the Mulla's allowances. To this a reply was given which it may be hoped satisfied the petitioners. It was to the effect that Government did not issue definite orders one day and cancel them the next. On this rebuff Mulla Powinda once more went to Kabul. In his absence the autumn (of 1910) passed quietly and in December an enormous jirga, at which between 7,000 and 8,000 men were present, attended at Jandola to consider the redistribution of the tribal allowances. Once again the idea was, working upon the basis of the tribal share of each section, to leave the distribution of the sum available to those concerned and after new lists of sectional maliks had been made out, the allowances were paid out accordingly.

Chapter VI

On his return from Kabul, Mulla Powinda renewed his efforts to form a Mahsud-Wazir alliance and a joint jirga actually came off at Kaniguram at which he and Sadde Khan, Madda Khel, were the protagonists. No permanent results were however secured. For the rest, the winter months passed without untoward incident, Mahsuds in large numbers being honestly employed on the Gumal road, the Bannu-Kalabagh Railway and the Moghal Kot road in Zhob. In March 1911 a chance encounter occurred in the Tiarza Nullah between members of the tribe and a militia patrol. This having resulted in casualties to the latter, the Mahsuds returned the captured rifles and paid up blood money in full without undue pressure. When the tribal allowances were paid at the spring jirga, all outstanding cases had been settled, recruiting for the army was brisk and the Mahsuds were themselves arranging a settlement with the Ghazni outlaws which would enable them to return to Mahsud country and resume their normal place in the tribal organisation. In July 1911 the Mulla again visited Kabul. His first reception by Sirdar Nasrullah Khan, the Amir's brother, through whom negotiations with the frontier tribes were generally conducted, was extremely unfavourable. The explanation given in contemporary reports is only that Muhammad Akbar Khan, Shahgassi of Khost, with whom the Mulla had fallen out, had been beforehand with him and denounced him to the Sirdar as a double faced rogue who, while posing as a ghazi and the inveterate enemy of the British Government and drawing allowances from Kabul on the strength of these pretensions, was in reality selling his country to the British and allowing his near relatives to take contracts on the roads which Government with his support was making in Mahsud country. From this attack Mulla Powinda only saved himself by the sworn testimony of Sadde Khan, who was also visiting Kabul, and took oath that no roads at all were being made in Mahsud country.

But it seems probable that the Afghans really were unfavourably impressed by what they heard of Government's activities in the development of communications on the Waziristan border and by the recent occupation of the Thal-Idak line by the Tochi Militia, and the quarrel between the Mulla and the Shahgassi may well have been occasioned by his supposed acquiescence in these measures and not by merely personal antipathy. Any how he saved himself, and his allowances of Rs. 7,000 and 2,000 cartridges were restored. Their allowances were also paid to the maliks who had followed him to Kabul. But before their departure they were given to understand that they would in future be expected to earn their keep by working in with the Shahgassi, preventing the construction of any roads in Mahsud country and by stopping recruitment for the Indian army. Consequently on his return the Mulla adopted a less ambiguous attitude. He allowed his shaikhs to commit two dacoities with murder in the Dera Ismail Khan District, did his best to draw away the Mahsuds working on the Bannu-Kalabagh Railway, whither the pressure of a very lean autumn harvest had driven them in large numbers, and started preaching open hostility to Government. All the while he was in constant communication with the Shahgassi and with Mulla Hamzullah of Shakai. He then summoned a jirga to Kaniguram and with the support of three important Palli Khel maliks, who had been with him to Kabul, collected a lashkar and basing it on Nanu and Barwand endeavoured to organise an attack *en masse* on Sarwakai post. The news of this brought the Chief Commissioner on the scene with the Dera Ismail Khan Brigade at his heels. The bulk of the tribe were not behind the Mulla and no considerable section had any desire for war. The lashkar consequently broke up as soon as it was seen that Government was in earnest and general relief was felt and *more Mahsudico* expressed when the bluff was called and the tribe let off with a fine of Rs. 10,000 and a warning of their responsibility for the Mulla's actions. The fine was paid within a fortnight, but the unrest thus aroused produced the usual aftermath of raids, both in the Dera Ismail Khan District and in the Tochi Agency. Two serious dacoities with kidnapping in the Tank sub-division were the work of Nana Khel sections (Abdur Rahman Khel and Nekzan Khel) and one similar offence in Daur country of the Abdullais. In each case sectional baramptas, as usual, brought about a prompt and satisfactory settlement.

In October 1909 Captain Patterson had been succeeded as Political Agent, South Waziristan, by Captain James, who however only remained until the following May. A new departure was then made by the appointment of Major Dodd, who was not a member of the Political Department, but a military officer with a long and remarkable record of service with the Waziristan Militias. At first he retained the post of Commandant, South Waziristan Militia, and was Political Agent in addition.

In August 1912 Mulla Powinda once again paid the visit to Kabul which had now become an annual affair. The disturbances in Khost led by the Ghilzai Jahandad Khan had just come to an end and had resulted in the removal of the Shahgassi Muhammad Akbar Khan. Perhaps in consequence of this, perhaps on the strength of his exploits in the Sarwakai region, he and his following of maliks were this time able to secure their allowances without difficulty. The Mulla even extracted an additional douceur of Rs. 1,000 and returned in great fettle, announcing that in future Government would never embark on operations against the Mahsuds without the previous consent of the Amir. Quarrels between his own relatives however absorbed much of his energy for some months after his return and it was not until the spring that he had leisure for outside affairs of greater moment. Intolerable raiding in the Tochi Agency, Bannu, and Kohat Districts by gangs from Khost during the years 1907 onwards had induced the Government of India in 1910–11 to reoccupy the Lower Tochi posts with regulars and send the Militia thus released to Spinwam and Shewa on the Thal-Idak line, thus cutting across the raiders' main route. The Militia posts thus established were not withdrawn and were of course connected by some sort of track with their base.

The move was bitterly resented in Kabul, and it is difficult not to connect it with the Mulla's unfavourable reception there of the year in which it took place and not to trace a parallel between the Kabul Khel rising of 1913 and that of the Madda Khel in 1897, with Mulla Powinda behind the scenes on both occasions. We learn that in February 1913 he embarked upon very active correspondence with the new Hakim of Khost and shortly after went suddenly himself to Matun. He was actually in Khost when the Kabul Khel outbreak took place. Shortly before this a dacoity with murder had occurred near Mullazai in the Dera Ismail Khan

District in which Shabi Khel Mahsuds of the Mulla's following took the leading part. Immediately after the Kabul Khel outbreak, which unlike the Maizar affair of 1897 achieved no initial success and was promptly dealt with by troops, the Mulla returned from Khost and, after sending in a deceitful letter to the Political Agent of which no notice was taken, set about rousing the tribes of Waziristan with rumours of Afghan action, prompted by events in the Balkans, and other inflammatory stuff. The Mullazai dacoity had been countered by a fairly successful Shabi Khel barampta and, in the prevailing excitement, advantage was taken of the lever thus afforded to get as many Mahsuds of importance as possible into Tank and there inoculate them against the virus spread by the Mulla. This move was claimed as a brilliant tactical manoeuvre, though the advantages of withdrawing influential maliks at such a time seems questionable. Anyhow the tribe as a whole remained tranquil. What is more, the Shabi Khel barampta turned many of his own section against the Mulla and adversely affected his tribal position. The tribe itself did nothing very serious, but we read that about this time the Abdur Rahman Khel outlaws from Ghazni, with whom no settlement had ever been made by the other Mahsuds, committed no less than five 'outrages' of which the most serious were an attack on a party of the 72nd Punjabis on 13 May between Nili and Khajuri Kach, and a similar offence in Zhob. In the Khajuri Kach affair three sepoys were killed and two rifles carried off, the raiders losing one man, a notorious raider named Musa Khan. In Zhob five Militia sowars were killed and five rifles carried off. These the outlaws took to Afghanistan where they were actually purchased by Mulla Powinda and were subsequently recovered from the Mahsuds.

As soon as the failure of his schemes was apparent the Mulla once more went to Kabul, where we may suppose that he put himself right with the authorities, but he made no long stay. For in June we find him back again and spending the rest of the summer in a dramatic but ineffectual attempt to settle the old feud between the Zargar Khel Wazirs of the Tochi and the Manzar Khel. In this he was backed by Mulla Hamzullah of Shakai, who was perhaps in even closer touch with the Afghan authorities than he was, and it is hard not to see in it, first, another bid for a super-tribal position by Mulla Powinda and second, the dictates of Afghan policy. In pursuit of this idea Mulla Powinda after a joint jirga at Kaniguram took a considerable number of Mahsuds with him to Wazir country, but on its way back *re infecta* the party was attacked, near where Razmak camp now stands, by the Tori Khel Wazirs and the combatants did not separate until each side had lost about twenty men killed. This happened early in August and as a result of it the Mahsuds remained in occupation of Razmak for some months, after which they permitted the Tori Khel to return on certain conditions, one being that they should build no 'kots'. Towards the end of October Mulla Powinda fell seriously ill and on 2 November he died. Mulla Powinda cannot have been more than fifty years old, but there is no reason whatever for supposing that his death was due to any but natural causes. Nevertheless even a decade later, as I can testify from personal knowledge, the belief among the Mahsuds that he had been removed by poison was by no means extinct. At the time of his death this rumour was very strong. The poison was supposed to have been administered by his eldest son, Sahib Din, who fled to Tank immediately upon his father's death. The design was generally attributed to the same Political Tahsildar of whose personal influence over Muhammad Jan, the Abdur Rahman Khel raider, mention has already been made. This same Muhammad Jan, whose name does not appear in the crimes register after his reformation in 1910, though his section retained their old evil prominence, also met his end this year. He was murdered in Tank by a Bhitanni, brother of a Militia Jemadar who had met his death while in pursuit of a gang under Muhammad Jan, and here again current gossip in the Agency traced, and still traces, the working of the same hidden hand. These rumours in the light of after events are not without significance.

Mulla Powinda's character cannot be judged by any standards current amongst Englishmen. By these he must be set down quite simply in Lord Curzon's phrase as a 'first class scoundrel'. But by those who have made allowances for the environment in which he lived, he cannot be denied some tribute of admiration as a determined and astute, though not altogether single-minded, patriot and champion of his tribe's independence. All officers who ever actually met him will agree that his forceful character, striking appearance, and persuasive eloquence made a deep impression on those with whom he came into personal contact. A man who, without any inherited advantages and without education, could make so large an instalment of frontier history in effect but a series of chapters in his own biography, can have been no little man, and given more malleable metal to work upon than Mahsuds have ever afforded and a more fortunate setting in time and place, he might well have ranked with many who are accounted great men. His death was a great blow to the Mahsuds and the selection of a successor was accounted a matter of national concern for which a great jirga was held at Kaniguram. Mulla Hamzullah presided, but the leading part was played by Mulla Abdul Hakim, a Mahsud of the Malikdinai section, who had for years been Mulla Powinda's confidential secretary and the Political Agent's chief source of information as to his plans and doings. This worthy read out to the assembled Mahsuds the farewell letter to his countrymen in which Mulla Powinda gave them some excellent advice. He exhorted them to hold their nationality intact and allow neither the British Government nor the Amir to encroach upon their country, to compose their internal differences, and to give up raiding, so as to deprive Government of a convenient excuse for occupying Mahsud country. Finally he commended to them his second surviving son, Fazal Din, a boy of about fourteen, as his successor. The bequest was honoured without serious opposition, and all real power at once passed into the hands of Mulla Abdul Hakim, who completely dominated the immature Fazal Din.

But Abdul Hakim could not hope to maintain his position indefinitely. He was indeed compelled to carry on Mulla Powinda's policy and his only chance of doing so with success and of remaining himself at the helm was to act in far more spectacular and violent fashion than the Mulla himself had done. In short his sole chance lay in embroiling the Mahsuds with Government. This he appears to have been intelligent enough to perceive.

The prestige of the departed leader is sufficiently illustrated by an incident which occurred in February 1914, four months after his death. A dispute had arisen between the Shaman Khel on the one side and the Abdur Rahman Khel on the other regarding lands in Spli Toi. The Shaman Khel were backed by the Alizai and the Abdur Rahman Khel by their brother Bahlolzai. The matter being one of importance neither side was prepared to give way. But neither side wished to fight, and so they agreed to leave the matter to the arbitration of Fazal Din. Thus was seen the whole Mahsud nation hanging on the word of an unproved stripling. This word Fazal Din left to himself would probably have given and thus irretrievably ruined his own position, but Abdul Hakim managed to stave off decision until other and more pressing affairs claimed Mahsud attention.

The diversion which may fairly be ascribed to him was not long in coming and when it came was no ordinary matter. Major Dodd had now been Political Agent, South Waziristan, for nearly four years on end and, as might be expected of such a man, had established his personal influence as a force to be reckoned with amongst the Mahsuds. According to the custom of the Agency he had a number of Mahsud orderlies. A good specimen of the Mahsud tribe, as indeed of other transborder tribes, so employed is very apt to be spoiled by his master. He is generally a brave man and in addition so deft, intelligent and useful, and very often so witty that he gets his own way far too much. This remark may be tested by observation in any Frontier Agency at almost any time. Such a one there now was amongst Major Dodd's entourage, a Malikshahi of good family named Sarfaraz. He had served for a short time with Major Dodd in the Tochi Scouts and had now been his personal orderly for four years. His duties were nominal and his pay handsome. He received every sort of kindness and favour and could get as much leave as he wanted for the asking. Of this privilege he availed himself during 1913–14 to an almost incredible extent and it was afterwards learned that while on leave he spent a great deal of time closeted with Fazal Din and Abdul Hakim both at Marobi and in Spli Toi, whither the latter had gone in connection with the dispute above mentioned. It will be remembered that at one time Mulla Powinda made something of a speciality of incitement to the murder of British officers and had scored three notable successes in this line. His methods must have been well known to Abdul Hakim and his recipes amongst the *arcana imperii* left to his successor. We must remember too that it was generally believed that he had been poisoned. Fazal Din, commonly called Shahzada, no doubt believed it; probably believes it still. There can be little room for doubt as to the nature of these conversations at Marobi and in Spli Toi. But it was not Fazal Din and Abdul Hakim only who were charged with complicity in the events which followed. The Abdur Rahman Khel connected with Muhammad Jan believed the rumour as to the machinations by which he had been removed and were also out for blood. One of them a man named Haibat, half brother of Muhammad Jan, is mentioned as having laid an ambush for the Political Agent in which he was himself killed by a Militia patrol. This had happened in the previous January, and no doubt had put another notch in the Abdur Rahman Khel tally against Major Dodd.

Whether the two sets of malcontents were aware of one another's intentions and were working in collusion is a point on which opinions might, and did, differ. Mr Donald, now officiating as Chief Commissioner, thought it inevitable. The local officers could find no proof of it. But whether this was so or not, there seems no reason to doubt that the two strands of crime were being twisted together for their own purposes by Fazal Din and his mentor. On 11 April Major Dodd's orderly Sarfaraz returned to Tank from his fifth leave of absence since the previous December. On arrival he learnt that a cheque for Rs. 339 for work done on the Gumal road, in which he had some share, had been stopped by Major Dodd's order, because the parties or persons connected with them were suspected of complicity in an affair of sheep stealing. During the course of the 12th Sarfaraz twice tried to get Major Dodd to cancel this order, but without success. The second attempt was made at 6 p.m. At 7.20 p.m. after the officers at Tank had finished their evening game of tennis and were sitting outside the political bungalow, Sarfaraz, having made every possible preparation to do as much damage as he could and to secure his own escape after doing it, opened fire on them with a magazine carbine—the gift of Major Dodd—at short range from a well-chosen place of concealment in the hedge of the political garden. There is no need to describe what happened in detail. Let it suffice to place on record that two British officers, Captain Brown of the South Waziristan Militia and Lieutenant Hickie, Royal Artillery, and three men of the Frontier Constabulary were killed on the spot; Major Dodd was mortally wounded and two chowkidars, one of them a Mahsud, also wounded by gunshot fire, before Sarafaraz was himself shot down.

News of this crime of course reached Mahsud country at once. It produced the effect which disturbing events on the frontier always produce—a crop of raids and other offences. Before the end of May six such had occurred in the Dera Ismail Khan District and ten in South Waziristan and Zhob, in nearly all of which the Abdur Rahman Khel took a leading part. On 16 May the officiating Chief Commissioner saw the Mahsud jirga at Tank and announced the orders of Government in respect of Major Dodd's murder. These were the surrender within a reasonable time of three male relatives of Sarfaraz for detention during the pleasure of Government and of three named Abdur Rahman Khel tribesmen to stand their trial on a charge of conspiracy against Major Dodd's life. The surrender of Fazal Din and Abdul Hakim was not demanded, for fear lest this should lead to an impasse which Government desired to avoid. Failing compliance with the demands actually made the tribal allowances were to be stopped. The summer passed with offences still continuing, and on the outbreak of the Great War these demands remained unfulfilled.

Chapter VII

The eve of the outbreak of the Great War seems an appropriate time for digressing to complete the record of Mahsud service in the Indian Army. As has been told, in 1910, mainly for political reasons, the Mahsud quota was raised from two to ten Companies, each a hundred and fourteen strong, distributed between four battalions. There was no difficulty over recruiting and by April 1911 'four embryo native officers and a hundred and fifty men had been sent' to the selected units—these of course in addition to the two already established companies. By next year 'the experiment of enlisting on a large scale Mahsuds for service in the regular army' is pronounced by the Chief Commissioner to have 'proved a great success'. The supply of recruits of the best stamp is described as almost inexhaustible and the Mahsud once away from home and priestly influences is said to have made 'a good and reliable soldier in whose praise Commanding officers are loud'. In 1913 a slightly less exultant note is struck. We learn that while enlistment as a whole had been progressing steadily, in one regiment there had been an unfortunate set-back. The Commanding Officer without knowing, or perhaps without caring, for the enormity of such a thing in Mahsud eyes, promoted a Palli Khel Non-Commissioned Officer in place of a Giddi Khel Jemadar. From his own point of view he may have been perfectly right, but his action resulted in the whole Giddi Khel complement taking their immediate discharge, and it was consequently severely commented on by political critics. Here it may be of interest to quote the opinions of some regimental officers. One writes 'The -th never enlisted Mahsuds till May 1912, when recruiting for three companies was started, two Manzais and one Mula (? Michi) Khel. These companies were more or less up to strength early in 1914. They were mostly sent as reinforcements to the 129th Baluchis in France, who reported well on their fighting capacity. They were however a constant source of trouble, in this Battalion at any rate, from the time recruiting started, until they finally left the Regiment'. From another unit, which also had three companies, it is reported 'unfortunately the

142

Mahsuds gave a certain amount of trouble on the outbreak of the war. One of the chief causes of the trouble was that the senior Subadar in the battalion was a direct Commission Mahsud,[1] who was comparatively young for his seniority (he only had about ten years' service) and when a vacancy for Subadar-Major occurred he was passed over by an Afridi'.

'On the 20th November 1914 when the Battalion was embarking for service overseas, Major N.R. Anderson was murdered on the quay by a Mahsud (Bahlolzai, Urmur Khel); the murderer was tried by Summary General Court Martial and hanged on the 22nd November 1914'.

From the 124th, which never had more than one company comes a much more favourable opinion. 'The Company did very good work indeed in the Battalion. Their quickness always gave them the right to represent the Battalion at Drill competitions, bayonet and sword events at the Assault at Arms. Only on one occasion before the war was there ever a loss of arms—one sentry going over the Border with his rifle. In 1915 the Pathan Company was ordered to France to join the 129th Baluchis. The Mahsuds strongly objected to leaving the Battalion and went reluctantly. However they fought extremely bravely in France. (Later) the Mahsuds, reinforced by all the recruits that had accumulated at the Depot, were sent with the 129th to East Africa. There their work was exceptionally good'.

By common consent those Mahsuds who actually reached the firing line in France and served with the 129th behaved magnificently, and I have heard an officer who commanded a Mahsud company later in the war in East Africa become almost lyrical in their praise. It was this same officer whose chance presence at Kotkai in 1920 seriously dislocated the progress of the Mahsud campaign, because so many of the enemy wanted to come in to see him. Despite their gallantry in the field the Mahsuds had no desire to display their heroism to the world and those who could get out of going to the front did so. Of one hundred and forty-two men called up on mobilisation only thirty-eight responded; recruits were not forthcoming and desertions actually occurred from regimental recruiting parties as well as from all border cantonments. In November 1914 the enlistment of Mahsuds was suspended and the same order soon afterwards was applied to all other transborder Pathans. At the end of the war all Mahsuds received their discharge and they have not been enlisted since.

---

1. Hayat Khan, Michi Khel, Palli Khel, Manzai, Alizai.

But with such entities as the frontier tribes the record of those who stayed at home is perhaps almost as important as that of those who went on service. To the question what he did in the Great War the Mahsud, on the home front as well as abroad, like the Afridi, must return a curiously unequal answer. He cannot indeed claim any such prodigy as the Qambar Khel Afridi brothers, Mir Mast and Mir Dast.[1] But Subedar Turkistan, Salimi Khel, of the leading family of the tribe, for example, who was twice wounded in France, is the younger brother of Malik Qutab, whose whole life is a record of ineffectual halting between two opinions. Nor is Turkistan the only Mahsud who played a man's part in the field, while his brothers and cousins played the fool elsewhere. A remarkable number of Mahsuds gained decorations for acts of gallantry in the field, but, as we have seen, their tribal record was disgraced by at least an equal number of outrageous military misdemeanours which made their exclusion from the Indian Army, in the circumstances then obtaining, nothing but an act of common prudence, as they themselves recognise. When deploring the loss to their countrymen of military service Mahsuds not uncommonly sum up the discussion with the remark *'Mizh der beitabora khalq yi'*.[2] God knows, that is true enough. It is never easy to predict what any Mahsud is going to do next and never was this national trait more prominent than during the war years both at home and in the field.

---

1. Mir Mast deserted in France to the enemy. He had the rank of Jemadar and the Germans made much of him. It is said that they even gave him the Iron Cross. After various adventures he reached Tirah with the Turkish Mission and there made much mischief. Mir Dast won the Victoria Cross in France. Mir Mast is now dead.
2. 'We are very untrustworthy people'.

Chapter VIII

So then when the fateful news of 4 August 1914 reached the frontier the Mahsuds at once realised that the situation was likely to tie the hands of Government and the Political Agent (Mr T. B. Copeland, I.C.S., who had taken over charge after Major Dodd's murder) received a number of threatening letters sent with the intention to test whether Government were likely to recede from the terms announced in May. Early in September a Mahsud deputation of unusual size and importance, which included Fazal Din and Mulla Abdul Hakim, paid the annual visit to Kabul where their arrival coincided with that of a number of Ahmedzai Wazir malcontents headed by Mulla Hamzullah. Both groups were received by Nasrullah Khan with marked respect and the Mahsuds at least were treated with hitherto unprecedented liberality. They were paid Rs. 21,500 and after both sides had been exhorted to dwell together in harmony they were permitted to depart. The magnitude of the sums given to them naturally aroused the covetousness of those who had not gone and throughout the autumn strenuous but unsuccessful efforts were made to induce Government to re-open allowances to those maliks and sections whose behaviour was not at fault. While this matter was being discussed in jirga at Tank with the officiating Chief Commissioner, Fazal Din's party were making great efforts to tempt the tribe to a serious outbreak, and an opposition meeting was held at Kaniguram, which was attended by the firebrand mulla from Khost known as Lala Pir. All Lala Pir's zeal however could not atone for his blunders. There is scarce one of the old errors which he did not commit. He tried to get the Mahsuds to endorse a petition to the Amir to take over their country; he tried to settle the question of the 'kots' at Razmak, and he set about drawing up a list of approved recipients of Kabul allowances. It is not surprising that immediately after this the Mahsuds razed to the ground four 'kots' which the Wazirs had built at Razmak and Lala Pir left the country. The Mahsuds took no part in the Tochi disturbances of January 1915, but in February Fazal Din actually started to raise a lashkar with the avowed intention of attacking Tank. This came to nothing, but though the tribe did not venture to risk the grand coup, numerous members of it were having great fun with smaller stakes. In the previous administrative year (April 1913–March 1914) the Mahsuds had been responsible for thirty-one offences 'of some importance' which included twelve cattle liftings and four cuttings of telegraph wires. In the twelvemonth [year] which witnessed the murder of Major Dodd and the first eight months of the war period, the tale of their misdeeds, from which cattle lifting, burglary, and wire cutting, all numerous, are now excluded, had risen to eighty-one, in three of which they had some assistance from Bhitannis. In these, twenty-eight persons were killed by them, and twenty-four wounded and nine Hindus were kidnapped. Nearly all the crime was the work of the Shabi Khel and of various Nana Khel sections with, of course, the Abdur Rahman Khel at their head. The comparative abstinence of other sections from this orgy is to be accounted for by other motives besides unmitigated virtue. Ever since the destruction of the Tori Khel towers at Razmak in the previous autumn tribal relations between Mahsuds and Utmanzai Wazirs had been very strained. In the spring of 1915 Mahsuds reaped the Wazir crops and sowed the lands themselves for autumn. Both sides then collected considerable forces. A few shots were fired but peace was soon patched up, partly through the efforts of Afghan delegates. By the terms of it the Wazirs were allowed to destroy five Mahsuds towers at Spinkamar and to re-occupy Razmak on the same terms as before. Both sides were then about to start for Kabul, but were prevented by an outbreak of cholera.

The sections of the Mahsuds who are most concerned with Razmak belong to the Aimal Khel branch of the Bahlolzai, and it was they who were responsible for carrying out the first of the demands announced in connection with Major Dodd's murder. Over this Mr Copeland had a certain amount of luck. One of the men wanted fell into his hands about the time when the demand was presented and in the spring of 1915 the other two were surrendered. This cleared accounts with the Aimal Khel. Of the Abdur Rahman Khel suspects the most important, Brag by name, had meanwhile been killed in a tribal quarrel. The surrender of the officers remained as far off as ever and the tale of Mahsud crime, for which as usual Nana Khel Bahlolzai and Shabi Khel Alizai were chiefly responsible, was mounting to remarkable totals. The brew of the preceding years had been bitter but it was pop to what the Mahsud made us swallow in 1915–16. In that year a hundred and eighty offences of a kind to be classed as serious were committed by Mahsuds with or without help from other tribes. Amongst their victims or those opposed to them, a hundred persons lost their lives, seventy were wounded, and ninety-three unfortunates, chiefly Hindus, were kidnapped. Seldom can any political officers have been called upon to grapple with a more difficult situation than that which confronted those responsible for the conduct of relations with the Mahsuds. With the Great War in progress and large Indian contingents sanguinarily engaged overseas, it was naturally Government's prime object, wherever possible, to avoid tribal hostilities. But the local situation was one which called, indeed clamoured, for the use of force. Afghan intrigue, as we have seen, was rife. The tribal allowances had been stopped over Major Dodd's murder and their continued stoppage, though inevitable, deprived the Political Agent of his chief means of control. It was a grievance to the well-behaved sections and it did not repress the more turbulent. For a variety of reasons raiding was unusually safe and profitable. So the beam gradually rose against the Political Agent until in October 1915 a tribal jirga held at Kaniguram under the nominal presidency of Fazal Din actually ventured to present an ultimatum demanding, amongst other things, the restoration of allowances and the release of the interned Mahsuds belonging to the 130th Baluchis, with a fortnight's time limit for compliance. The period expired, amid great tribal excitement, without sign from Government. There followed two exploits rather of war than of brigandage. On 18 November 1915 some picquets near Khajuri Kach held by the 45th (Rattray's) Sikhs were attacked by a large gang of Mahsuds, chiefly Abdur Rahman and Shabi Khel. In this affair five sepoys were killed, and one British officer and nine sepoys wounded. Eleven days later another picquetting party of the South Waziristan Militia was ambushed near Tormandu and ten sepoys killed, three wounded, and thirteen rifles carried off. The response to these stimuli was an order for barampta of all Mahsuds wherever found and for the whole tribe to be held under blockade. This and the signal failure of a large raid by Manzai sections at the village of Shaikh Sultan, in which eight Mahsuds were killed, produced a lull, but it did not last long. By March (1916) Mullas and Afghan agents were once more conspicuously active and Mahsud raiding by large gangs as bad as ever it had been in the preceding year. The Viceroy in a public speech delivered on 24 March announced that 'the cup of their (the Mahsuds') misdeeds was already overflowing and the day of retribution only delayed till our pre-occupations elsewhere should be relieved'. A few days later Kut fell, and the pre-occupations of the Government of India so far from being relieved must have become more pressing than ever. The local situation also developed, and the month of April 1916 saw no less than seventeen Mahsud raids in the Dera Ismail Khan District alone, the most serious of which was the ambushing of a Frontier Constabulary patrol party in the Zarwani pass near Manjhi, in which seven sepoys were killed, two wounded, and eleven rifles taken. Consequently in May another Mahsud barampta was ordered, and the measure of success achieved by this reveals how ineffective had been the blockade declared only a few months previously. By this means a settlement of some kind was patched up with the better disposed sections[1] and they were permitted to resume commercial relations. The tribe was thus split into two camps and at the autumn tribal jirga Fazal Din's claim to represent the Mahsud nation was definitely repudiated and an intimation to that effect sent to Kabul. This roused Fazal Din and the hostiles to fresh efforts. In December a lashkar was collected at Barwand to attack Sarwakai, but it dispersed without action. In February 1917 Fazal Din made a second attempt and by the production of letters from Kabul—whether genuine or not—secured better support. Hamzullah of course was there and a few Wazirs with Mahsuds of many sections, but chiefly Shabi Khel and Nana Khel. Sarwakai post was surrounded. The officer in command there (Major Hughes) finding his post heavily sniped thought proper to occupy Garesi Sar about 1,400 yards away with a detachment of one hundred men. This he had no difficulty in doing, but maintaining the detachment

---

1. Described as: Shaman Khel – the whole

Alizai	– Manzai	
Bahlolzai	– Nanakhel	Haibat Khel
	Jallal Khel	Umar Khel
	Kikarai	Aimal Khel
	Abdullai	Band Khel

and keeping it supplied with ammunition, rations, and water was a very different matter. After a few days he consequently decided to withdraw it and moved out in support with fifty men, leaving a hundred to garrison the post. This gave the Mahsuds their opportunity. They attacked at once and in the action which followed Major Hughes, two Indian officers and eighteen sepoys were killed, ten wounded, eleven taken prisoner, and thirty-eight rifles carried off. It was only by the gallantry and address of our old friend, the Afridi Subedar Mohibullah, that the remnant were saved. The rapid advance of a column from Tank however prevented further developments, the lashkar dispersed and Sarwakai was relieved without a shot being fired.

After burning some kirris near Barwand, with a loss of two men wounded only, the column withdrew to Khajuri Kach and having halted there for some days early in April began its retirement to Tank. Opposition at once revived. On 9 April two picquets between Khajuri and Nili Kach were ambushed. Twenty-four sepoys—militia and regulars—were killed, fifteen wounded, two taken prisoner, and twenty-six rifles carried off. Of the raiders three were killed. The departing columns were at once faced about and a strong force advanced up the Gumal to Wana and then camped at Tanai where it was within striking distance of Sarwakai, Wana, and the Gumal posts. Unfortunately it could not be maintained there without camel convoys constantly moving up and down, and the protection of convoys in such country, at which the old frontier regiments excelled, is a task for experts. On 1 May while a convoy of eighty camels was being escorted through the Ghwaleri Algad between Nili and Khajuri Kach an even more signal disaster than that of 9 April took place. It resulted in a loss of two British officers, two Indian officers, and fifty-one Indian other ranks killed, fifty-three wounded, and the loss of sixty-four rifles. The Mahsud loss was one man killed and one wounded. This put the fat in the fire. The whole tribe turned against Government and even the friendlies sent in an ultimatum. The tale of depredations in the border villages continued steadily to rise and Mahsud lashkars of considerable size were constantly on the prowl in regions where a brush might be expected. On 10 May a fierce encounter took place between the Khuzhma Sar and Sarwakai. In this the troops were the aggressors, though they had ultimately to retire, and the fortune of war more equal. The losses were, on the one side, two British officers, one Indian officer, and thirty-six ranks and file killed, sixty-three wounded, and seventy missing; on the other, seventy Mahsuds killed, including the notorious leader Sher Dil, Abdur Rahman Khel. One hundred and twenty-three rifles were however lost. Yet another, though smaller, picquetting disaster took place on 16 May between Nili and Khajuri Kach in which one British officer and eighteen men were killed, nine wounded, and twenty-five rifles lost. Two days later a mixed lashkar of Mahsuds and Wazirs led by Mulla Hamzullah, of which the strength was estimated at 1,500 men, made an attack on the militia post at Wana, but the attack was not serious and was beaten off without loss. Very different was the next affair. On 31 May, by an exploit worthy of Robin Hood, Musa Khan, Abdullai, with six companions, two of whom were disguised as girls, secured possession of Tut Narai post in the Tochi, killing six and wounding eight of the small garrison. Having been joined by a lashkar outside the raiders got away with fifty-nine rifles and 8,000 rounds of ammunition, with a loss on their side of about a dozen men killed. It is noteworthy that the two members of the gang who were in feminine disguise were ex-soldiers of the North Waziristan Militia, of which the Mahsud company had first been given leave *en masse* at the time of the Sarwakai incident and then disbanded. Government's hand being thus forced, despite the time of year and all other objections, military action against the tribe was decided upon. As commonly happens, boldness was its own reward and the casualties of the expedition through enemy action sustained while biting the cherry did not equal those of the previous months of nibbling. The fact of the matter was that the mere appearance of two strong brigades, each with a British Territorial battalion and supported by such novelties as aeroplanes and Lewis guns, proved to the tribe by ocular demonstration that Government, for all its efforts overseas, still had a kick left in it for its enemies on the frontier, and did much to bring the tribe to their senses. Perhaps an even more important factor was the thoroughly unsympathetic attitude of His Majesty the Amir of Afghanistan, whom the Government of India had throughout kept informed of developments and consulted as to the best means of securing the peace of their common frontier. Even before the troops had entered Mahsud country His Majesty had taken the unprecedented step of informing the Mahsuds that none of their Kabul allowances would be paid so long as they were at war with Government. Whatever the reason, the force, advancing from Jandola by the Shahur route, was able to penetrate as far as Torwam in the Khaisara and carry out punitive operations at Nanu and elsewhere with far less opposition than the three Mahsuds can put up when their heart is in the business.

At the request of friendly maliks hostilities were suspended on 26 June and by the end of August the terms imposed, which were severe, had been complied with. These included:

1. the return of all rifles taken since 1 March 1917,
2. and of all prisoners without ransom,
3. the surrender for trial according to tribal custom or expulsion of all outlaws from British territory,
4. the surrender for trial according to tribal custom of Mirza Khan and Sher Dad, Abdur Rahman Khel, whose surrender had been demanded in 1914 on a charge of abetment of the murder of Major Dodd,
5. guarantees for future good behaviour.

At a big jirga held at Sarwakai in August peace was concluded. The two suspects stood their trial and were acquitted. Of the three hundred and eighty-six rifles demanded two hundred and ninty-one were handed back and equivalents given for the remainder. In return Government agreed to restore the tribal allowances with effect from 1 September 1917, to release all Mahsud political prisoners and detenus, except the men of the 130th Baluchis, and not to undertake the building of any new road or post in Mahsud country during the continuance of the settlement. This last condition is remarkable, but that it was well worth while is shown by a comparison of the statistics of Mahsud crimes and damages for the remaining years of the war. For convenience sake the figures of the preceding war years are repeated in the table below:

Year	Number of offences classed as serious	Number of persons killed	Number of persons wounded	Number of persons kidnapped
1914–15	81	28	24	9
1915–16	99	100	70	93
1916–17	74	75	70	132
1917–18	31	227	163	27[1]
1918–19	14	5	2	20

These figures take no account of offences against property. The details on record are too vague to be of any value, but it may be taken that, in offences committed by Mahsuds, violence and robbery go together.

Mr Copeland had been replaced as Political Agent, Wana, in May 1916 by Mr Fitzpatrick, I.C.S., to whom the credit of the new settlement is mainly due. He was fortunate to have had the military besom put through the mess, and fortunate after the expedition was over, in having plenty of work on road construction in the Gumal and elsewhere with which to keep the Mahsuds out of mischief. But of course he was not at an end of all difficulties. When in March 1918 the Mahsuds came in to Tank—which in accordance with a new scheme they did not all at once but by sections in eleven groups—to take their allowances, the Abdur Rahman Khel, though adhering to the settlement, refused their share, which according to the tribal reckoning amounts to 1/42 of the whole. In May this section surrendered ten good rifles in satisfaction of Government's claims, but at the same time, mindful perhaps of former concessions, they demanded a special annual allotment of Rs. 6,000 in compensation for the loss of income from raiding. This impudent request was referred to the tribe as a whole with a warning that, if this section gave trouble, joint tribal responsibility would be strictly enforced. This resulted in a compromise, ratified at the autumn jirga, held at Nili Kach

---

1. The 1917–18 figures include casualties in the Tochi and Wana agencies in various encounters between Mahsuds and troops and Militia before the expedition. Omitting these the figures of district crime were:

    Serious offences 21, persons killed 22, wounded 22, kidnapped 21. There were no serious offences after the expedition.

in December 1918, by which the tribe agreed unanimously for one year only, in return for guarantees of good behaviour and the settlement of all outstanding cases, to surrender to the recalcitrant section the sum demanded out of monies earned from road contracts. In fulfilment of this surprising compact, which was understood on all sides to be capable of renewal in future years, the Abdur Rahman Khel handed up four .303 rifles due from them on account of the misdeeds of their Kabul outlaws and committed no further depredations during the cold weather. But this was not the only difficult question. The spring and autumn allowance jirgas of 1918 were the first to be held after an interval of four years, and as, was to be expected with a people who live as dangerously as the Mahsuds, there were many gaps in the list of recipients. It will be remembered that ever since the patchwork arrangement invented by Mr Johnston in 1903 to supersede Mr Merk's famous settlement after the blockade, the Mahsud allowances, aggregating Rs. 70,000 per annum, had been divided into two shares, *viz.*, tumani (Rs. 54,000) paid to tumani vakils, or sectional representatives, and maliki (Rs. 16,000) paid to the old maliks of Mr Bruce's dispensation. It had been Mr Johnston's intention, and Mr Crump's after him, that the maliks, or after their deaths, their heirs, should get themselves appointed as sectional tumani vakils.

But the process was naturally a slow one and the opposition between the tuman and the maliks fostered by Mulla Powinda had prevented any real progress being made with it. Advantage was now taken by Mr Fitzpatrick of this need for extensive revision to inaugurate (once again) a new scheme of distribution whereby, while the interests of the old maliks were secured for life, the two sets of payments should be merged into one and a body of really influential allowances holders evolved, by consent of the tribe in consultation with the Political Agent. Considerable progress is said to have been made with this at the December jirga, but much was to happen before the problem could be taken up again.

Chapter IX

On 6 April 1919 Mr Fitzpatrick made over charge to Major Crosthwaite and went off to enjoy a well-earned period of furlough. Scarcely had the new Political Agent assumed his responsibilities when the storm aroused by the third Afghan War (6–31 May 1919) was upon him. It was unfortunate that this should have burst before he had had time to pick up the ropes and still more unfortunate that at this juncture Government should have been without the great personal influence and sound political instinct of Sir John Donald, who during the cold weather had been allowed to go on leave preparatory to retirement and had not been replaced. But it may be doubted whether in the fact of the forces now liberated any ties would have held the Mahsuds.

A few petty offences, the acts of spoilt children, took place in the early part of April, but otherwise all was quiet, and on 24 April the new Political Agent returned to Wana from Sarwakai after fixing 17 May as the date on which the next Mahsud allowance jirga was to begin at that place. For the rest of the month his peace was only disturbed by repeated cuttings of the telegraph line, a sign to which no importance was attributed, and it was not until 5 May, the day before war was declared, that he learned of the imminence of serious trouble. On 9 May Afghan propaganda, in the form of letters and messages addressed to prominent Mahsuds and Wazirs, including Wazir officers of the two local militias, began. Some distribution of Mahsud allowances took place on the appointed dates, but attendance was very meagre and it was found impossible to get any pending cases settled. The Mahsud situation was clearly rocky and the Political Agent accordingly himself remained at Sarwakai to watch it, and sent his Indian Assistant, Khan Bahadur Muhammad Yar Khan, to Wana to keep an eye on the Wazirs. By 25 May events had elsewhere developed so unfavourably that the militia posts in the Upper Tochi were evacuated. On learning of this the Political Agent, in virtue of the discretion vested in him by the Chief Commissioner to be exercised in such a contingency, ordered the evacuation of all militia posts in his

Agency. This was carried out on the night of 26 May. The garrisons of Sarwakai and the lower Gumal posts were successfully, except for numerous Afridi and Wazir desertions, withdrawn to Murtaza; but at Wana and the upper posts, of which the garrisons were to retreat across the Gumal into the Zhob Agency, the treachery of the same and other transborder elements in the crops caused disaster. Four British officers and the Indian Assistant lost their lives; two British officers were wounded; the militia practically ceased to exist; 1,200, .303 rifles and 700,000 rounds of ammunition fell into the hands of the tribesmen and the forces of disorder were carried in pursuit of the gallant remnant, which still held together, far into Baluchistan. In this affair only individual Mahsuds took part. It occurred outside Mahsud country, and so, beyond paying a tribute to the magnificent courage and endurance displayed by the Commandant, Major Russell, and those who stood by him, it is not necessary to enter into details. So far as the Mahsud tribe was concerned the immediate result of the evacuation was to bring a lashkar under Fazal Din down to attack Jandola (held by regulars) and to start the ball of border depredations rolling with a zip far beyond all previous performances. Jandola was relieved without difficulty on 9 June, but further military action was needed to restore the situation. This at the time it was not possible to take, and the hot weather passed in a series of petty and inconclusive, though often fiercely contested, actions between the troops and other forces collected along the district borders and Mahsud and Wazir raiding parties.

On the evacuation the tribes of the Agency appear to have been put under blockade, though the exact date on which the order was given is not upon record. With whole villages being looted daily the economic weapon for a time had little effect and the amount of military success achieved in the numerous encounters which took place merely shows how greatly conditions had altered since Major Macaulay's day. The course of events should give food for thought to advocates of continued adherence to the old close border policy which had once given such good results. I do not propose to go into details of all that happened except for one incident, which throws some light on Mahsud psychology and their occasional fits of blood lust. It occurred on the night of 29 August in the Bannu District. A gang consisting principally of Shaman Khel returning from a raid in the Mianwali District of the Punjab, in which it had secured sixteen rifles from the local police, fell upon the camp of a Labour Corps near Gambila. No resistance to speak of was offered, yet twenty-six defenceless coolies were butchered and twenty wounded before the advent of troops and police compelled the raiders to withdraw. It is good to learn that they were chased back to the hills and suffered a loss of fifteen killed and two prisoners, besides other casualties from heat and exhaustion, before the pursuit was relinquished.

The armistice with Afghanistan was signed on 31 May, only five days after the evacuation of the posts. But Afghan wars are not like wars in Europe. The trouble only became serious when the war was over. Towards the end of June reports were received that an Afghan officer named Shah Daula, generally described as a Colonel or Brigadier, in defiance of the armistice terms had arrived in Wana with two guns and a couple of hundred men and occupied the keep. In July he attended a Mahsud jirga at Kaniguram and embarked on a campaign of propaganda, backed by gifts of money and ammunition, amongst the Mahsuds and Wazirs. In August, having been visited by a British aeroplane, he shifted his quarters from the keep to the tahsil. On 8 August peace was signed, but it was some time before the news reached Waziristan. When rumours of it began to trickle through, Shah Daula did his best to discredit them, declaring that the peace was only a temporary arrangement, that in the real peace amnesty for all Mahsuds and Wazirs would be included, that the British Government would cede all its possessions beyond the Indus to Afghanistan, and so forth. Meanwhile he toured to Sarwakai and the Gumal and enlisted volunteers to occupy the posts. The tribesmen were however becoming suspicious and towards the end of September he was compelled to take a deputation of Mahsud and Wazir maliks with him to Matun, where they met Nadir Khan, the Afghan Commander-in-Chief. Amongst the Mahsuds who accompanied him we read of Marwat, Shaman Khel, Mehr Dil, Mal Khel,[1] and Aziz Khan, Shingi; Hayat Khan, Michi Khel, *ex*-Subedar of the 130th Baluchis, who had been released at the end of the Great War, also went, as also of course did Fazal Din and Abdul Hakim. The last mentioned died in Matun, either of cholera or influenza, and thus brought his evil career to a close.

---

1. These two are described as 'staunch supporters of Shah Daula'.

Musa Khan, Abdullai, did not go; nor did Qutab Khan, son of Badshah Khan, Salimi Khel, nor his uncle Adam Khan. Indeed at this time these two led the peace party. Nadir Khan did his best to support Shah Daula's assertions, but as his hearers were not satisfied, he selected sixteen men out of the Mahsud deputation and took them, as well as a number of Wazirs, with him to Kabul, where they arrived in October.

They were received by the Amir in person with every mark of honour, thanked for their services, liberally rewarded, especially those militia officers who had been prominent in treachery, given medals, and filled with flattery. Under these influences they presented a petition to the Amir of which the purport undoubtedly was that he should take over their country. This brought his cards on to the table. The awkward fact could not be concealed that a peace had been concluded in which no mention of Mahsuds or Wazirs was made. In one way or another however the deputation was led to think that the peace was not intended to be permanent and in December they returned to their homes with their hopes but little dashed. While they were away Shah Daula returned to Waziristan and renewed his activities, the fruit of which was seen in the tale of Mahsud offences, which amounted to over one hundred raids in the six months ending on 31 October 1919. These pin pricks however were not without their use. For they seem to have helped to convince Government that, despite a number of sound reasons for making no further call upon the forces at their disposal, military action against the tribes of Waziristan must be taken. A force, composed entirely of Indian troops, was assembled under the Command of Major-General Climo, in whom chief political control, directly under the orders of the Government of India, was also vested. General Climo summoned the Mahsud jirga to Khirgi on 3 November to hear the terms which had been decided upon. Mr Barton had held the post of Resident in Waziristan from June to September 1919 but had then, when Sir Hamilton Grant succeeded Sir George Roos-Keppel as Chief Commissioner, been transferred out of the North-West Frontier Province, and the post of Resident, on his departure, once more remained unfilled. In the absence of a Resident the terms were announced to the jirga by Major Crosthwaite. They included nothing more terrible than a Rs. 10,000 fine, forfeiture of allowances pending proof of good behaviour, return of rifles, and other military equipment taken since 1 May, and an admission of Government's right to make roads, station troops, and build posts, in any manner and by any labour thought fit, wherever Government pleased in the 'Protected Area', including the Shahur route from Jandola to Sarwakai. The other demands were allowed by the Mahsuds to be reasonable, but this last term stuck in their gizzards. For, unlike the Gumal, the Shahur valley is an integral part of Mahsud country. With it occupied, their proudest boast would be gone. Gone too, as they full well knew and as subsequent experience has since proved to sceptical frontier experts, would be their safe high way to and from the district borders and their pleasant and profitable raiding parties into the Daman. So with a polite excuse that they would comply as soon as they heard that the Afridis had done the same, the Mahsuds on 11 November rejected the offer. Intensive air operations against them began on 13 November and continued for about a month, while the troops were busy with the Wazirs in the Tochi, but failed to effect their submission. Consequently on 18 December the striking force, consisting of two brigades under the command of Major-General Skeen, with Major Crosthwaite as Political Officer, began its advance from Jandola. The task committed to General Climo was the punishment of the Mahsuds, and it was thought that this could best be done by the penetration of a single column up the Takki Zam valley from Jandola towards Dwa Toi, where the Baddar joins the Takki Zam, from which point both Makin and Kaniguram are accessible. So this was the plan on which it acted.

An excellent account of the operations which ensued is already in existence, the work of the General Staff at Army Head Quarters, and it is unnecessary and would be foreign to the purpose of this monograph to tell the military story over again. The advance was opposed by a strong contingent of Wana Wazirs as well as by the Mahsuds in full force, and it was not until 16 February 1920 that Dwa Toi was reached and then only after[1] such fighting as had never before been seen on the frontier. All this time considerable elements in the tribe, notably the Shingis

---

1. The casualties sustained by the force were killed 366 (including 28 British and 15 Indian officers) missing 237 (including 1 British officer) wounded 1,683: total 2,286. What the Mahsud losses may have been is of course a matter of conjecture, but there can be little doubt but that they were at least equal to ours. The General Officer Commanding's own estimate was 650–700 killed and 1,000 wounded. A Haibat Khel malik once told me in conversation that his (comparatively insignificant) section lost

and others whose lands lay in the line of advance, had been talking of peace, and negotiations of a partial and desultory nature had from time to time taken place. There was still in fact a considerable peace party among the Mahsuds, but the disadvantages to which such must always be exposed, while fighting is still in progress, prevented them from making much headway against the propaganda of Shah Daula, whose presence in Waziristan, with his guns, his money, his supplies of ammunition and his men, and his assistants, Haji Abdur Razzak, formerly Court Chaplain to Nasrullah Khan and the late Amir, Mulla Hamzullah, and our friend Lala Pir once again, was naturally taken by the tribesmen as proof that they were not going to be left altogether in the lurch. But after the stubborn fight at Ahnai Tangi (9–14 January) and the fiasco at the Barari Tangi (23–28 January) in which Shah Daula's guns proved completely ineffective, the more intelligent began to perceive that the game was up. The Wazir contingent, who had suffered very heavily at Ahnai, returned to their homes. Shah Daula and Abdur Razzak went to Kaniguram and thence to Wana and Shakai. Fazal Din left for Marobi, just above Dwa Toi, to exhume the body of his lamented father, and the Mahsud lashkar began to break up. A few days after reaching Dwa Toi the force was in a position to begin punitive operations at Makin and now, to save their houses and towers there, the Umar Khel section of the Nana Khel Bahlolzai were the first to bring in twelve Government rifles, their share of the fine on the inhabitants of that place. Their property was accordingly spared, but, as the other sections failed to follow this example effectively, most of the other towers and houses in Makin were demolished, before the troops withdrew on 1 March to a camp afterwards known as Ladha on the Baddar, a few miles above Dwa Toi. On 6 March the column reached Kaniguram and settled down to a long halt. On 20 March the Shaman Khel, Manzai and Aimal Khel (less the Abdullais) had brought in a hundred and forty-eight Government and a hundred and seventy-eight tribal rifles, and a considerable proportion of the fine, thus saving Kaniguram from sharing the fate of Makin. On 21 March a jirga was held at which the Mahsuds were told that the troops would remain in their country at any rate until the autumn crop sowing season

---

40 men killed in these days. If all sections suffered proportionately this would mean a loss of between 1,500–2,000 killed in the whole tribe.

was over and that recalcitrant sections would be liable to sudden attack. Early in April in pursuance of this threat a force was sent to chastise the Abdur Rahman Khel and Giga Khel who live at the head of the Baddar valley on the borders of Shakai. It encountered no very serious opposition and returned to Kaniguram after two days. In May the whole column returned to Ladha, where a permanent camp had been constructed, and sat itself down. The position now was in effect one of stalemate. The Mahsuds as a whole were under blockade. Those sections whose lands lay in the Takki Zam, such as Shingis, Shabi Khel, and Shaman Khel had mostly submitted, paid their quota of the fine, and handed up the rifles demanded of them. But permission to return and cultivate their lands was necessarily accompanied by such stringent conditions, as in effect to prevent them from taking advantage of it. In consequence they were well nigh starving, while the Abdullais of Makin and Spinkamar, the Haibat Khel, Abdur Rahman Khel, Jallal Khel, and other recalcitrants living out of reach had surrendered nothing, lost nothing except men killed in battle, and were in undisturbed enjoyment of their homes.

In May 1920 Mr Fitzpatrick returned from leave and, taking over the double role of Resident and Political Agent, replaced Major Crosthwaite as political adviser to the Force Commander. At his instance at a jirga held at Ladha on 28 May the blockade was raised for those sections who had fully complied with the terms. This move at once changed the lot of the friendlies from derision to envy. Other sections speedily came in—even the Haibat Khel who paid up in July. By the end of the hot weather only the Abdullais, the Abdur Rahman Khel, the Jallal Khel, and the Band Khel remained in open hostility. In July 1920 General Matheson relieved General Climo and in the autumn, with the Mahsud situation quiescent, the new Force Commander was able to turn his attention to the Wana Wazirs. Brigadier Shah Daula indeed remained on in Waziristan till January 1921, but he suffered gradual eclipse by Haji Abdur Razzak, who had moved to Wana from Shakai in October and from Wana continued to fan the flames of opposition both amongst the Mahsuds and the Wazirs. It was undoubtedly largely due to his influence that attacks by hostile Mahsuds on the troops along the line of communications leading to Ladha and as well as raids into the Daman continued to be of frequent occurrence.

The Wana Wazirs perceiving that their turn was now coming applied to the Mahsuds for assistance in return for the help which they had given them in their hour of need. To this request the Mahsuds gave a characteristic reply. They said that but for Wazir support they would have made peace before the great fight at Ahnai Tangi and thus avoided much suffering and heavy losses. Therefore they owed the Wazirs no gratitude, but a grudge, and they refused all help. Not only this, but when the Wana column advanced through the Shahur to Sarwakai, they shephered them through, waived off their own hostiles, and finally, when Abdur Razzak with his Wazir Levy advanced to Sarwakai to make a stand there, the Manzai of Nanu and the tribes of the Khaisara turned him out of Sarwakai fort which they held till the arrival of the troops and indeed continued to garrison thereafter while the column remained at Wana.

In December 1920 the leading maliks of the tribe put forward a petition, the contents of which clearly showed that they realised the position; that they regarded the permanent occupation of their country as probable and were determined to safeguard tribal interests in that event, and that meanwhile they had forsaken overt opposition and taken to exploiting such opportunities as were presented by the local purchase of supplies and the initiation of the new policy of road construction, designed eventually to link up Jandola with the Tochi Agency.

This, except from the point of view of the Wana Wazirs, is the bright side of the picture, as painted by Mr Fitzpatrick, but, as he also pointed out, much still remained to be done. True, that out of a total of three hundred Government rifles, five hundred tribal rifles, and Rs. 10,000 fine, two hundred and forty-two Government rifles, two hundred and seventy-nine tribal, and Rs. 9,214 had by the spring of 1921 been collected. But the hostile sections, many members of whom, especially the Abdur Rahman Khel, had now received grants of land in Logar and elsewhere near Kabul and only visited their native country as winter migrants, were still giving endless trouble on the Ladha line. They made up in virulence what they lacked in numbers and remained as far from reconciliation as ever. Till they were dealt with no general settlement was possible, and the tribe could not settle down.

On the departure of Sir George Roos-Keppel in the autumn of 1919 a new method of preparing the annual reports was introduced and

from that year figures showing the amount of Mahsud depredations
in all areas are no longer available. Details of raids in the Bannu and
Dera Ismail Khan Districts are however on record, and in any year it is
fairly safe to assume that the lion's share of this damage has been done
by Mahsuds. For purposes of comparison and convenience of reference
the figures of all the remaining years to which this monograph extends,
are given below:

Year	Number of offences	Number of persons killed	Number of persons wounded	Number of persons kidnapped	Value of property carried off (in lakhs rupees)
1919–20	324	149	227	197	12.76
1920–1	233	106	125	188	1.66
1921–2	129	50	56	108	.81
1922–3	73	33	36	42	.42
1923–4	44	21	16	6	.34
1924–5	25	7	2	18	.06

Of the offences committed this year in the Dera Ismail Khan District,
one calls for remark. This was a raid committed on the night of 21/22
October on the military labour camp at Kaur Bridge, very near the spot
where Kaur Post now stands. It was the work of a mixed gang of Mahsuds
and Wana Wazirs. On this occasion, as at Gambila in the previous year,
the tribesmen gave way to senseless ferocity. One British officer, two
British soldiers, and thirty-seven camp followers and labourers were killed
and about the same number wounded. Twenty-six rifles and a number of
horses and mules were carried off.

In March 1921 Sir Hamilton Grant was succeeded as Chief Commissioner by Sir John Maffey, but since chief political control in
Waziristan still remained vested in the Force Commander, the change
made little difference in the local situation. No decision had yet been
reached as to future policy in Waziristan. The troops remained at Ladha.
The hostiles continued to prowl and pounce on the unwary wherever
opportunity offered on the lines of communication. The principles

of local and tribal responsibility were introduced and used to prevent
the repetition of these acts, but these principles at best are a passive
defence, and the difficulty of enforcing them amongst a tribe like the
Mahsuds, where sections live all higgledy-piggledy jumbled up together,
is very great. Accordingly in June more active measures were tried. A
systematic bombardment of Makin from Ladha camp was begun and
continued at intervals till September. The Abdullais of Makin then, in
the absence of Musa Khan who was away in Kabul, sued for peace and
accepted the terms, as also did the Band Khel and the Shingis of Warza.
These two sections speedily complied with the terms, but the Abdullais,
after delivering forty-nine out of the hundred and fifteen Government
rifles believed to be in their possession, hung fire and drifted back into
an attitude of passive resistance. Nevertheless the situation was slowly
improving, and to this improvement several factors contributed. The mere
lapse of time had its sedative effect; the good behaviour of the troops; the
payment of liberal compensation for land still occupied; road-making and
the provision of ample lucrative employment, not only as labourers—a
role for which the Mahsuds now showed no great taste, but on protection
duty and in the Khassadar force—the conclusion of a final treaty with
Afghanistan in February 1922, and the decline of active Afghan intrigue
amongst the Mahsuds—all these helped.

In August 1921 Major Parsons came as Political Agent to deal with
the Wana Wazirs and relieved Mr Fitzpatrick of that part of his dual
functions. In January 1922 Mr Fitzpatrick gave way as Resident to
Mr Pears, and Major Parsons then—Wana having meanwhile been
evacuated—took charge of the Mahsuds as well. But still the question of
policy was not decided; still the troops sat behind barbed wire at Ladha
and all down the line, and still incidents continued to occur, wherever
carelessness or inexperience gave the watchful hostiles an opening. The
new Resident let no grass grow under his feet. Within a month or two
of taking over charge he had formulated his proposals for enhanced
allowances to all the tribes of Waziristan and for Khassadar service. These,
though expensive, were sanctioned without delay by Government and
by May he was announcing them to the Wazirs of the Tochi and stating
in a formal declaration, which has become the Magna Charta of the
Utmanzai, the conditions on which, with the Wazirs' consent, Razmak

was to be occupied by the forces of Government. All through the summer road construction was pressed on with feverish haste and by December sufficient progress had been made to enable a force under Major-General Jacob to advance from the Tochi *via* Isha, Damdil, the Khaisora, Razani, and Razmak Narai to the Razmak plateau (known to the local tribes as Laghare[1] Raghza), where they encamped.

According to the traditional tribal reckoning the Utmanzai Wazirs of the Tochi muster 60,000 men. These tribes had behaved so well during the Great War that before the outbreak of the Afghan War proposals had actually gone forward for the doubling of their allowances. Under the new agreements negotiated by Mr Pears they accepted very much greater responsibilities than before. It was therefore only natural that their allowances should be augmented and the figure now fixed by Mr Pears, Rs. 72,000, though liberal, in addition to Khassadar service, was not excessive. The Mahsuds, whose traditional number is only 18,000 men, were already in receipt of nearly that amount for many years before the Great War. Throughout the Great War, as a tribe, they behaved exceedingly badly and the same responsibilities, which the Wazirs accepted willingly, were only forced upon them at the point of the sword. It must therefore be taken as a tribute to their military efficiency that their allowances were at the same time raised from Rs. 70,000 to Rs. 1,08,000, of which Rs. 60,000 were declared to be 'nikat', *i.e.* divisible according to the ancestral share of each section in tribal profit and loss, and the remainder 'khidmati', 'to be distributed equitably among the maliks and other representatives after due consideration of special services rendered—or any other factor meriting special adjustment'. The new allowances were announced at a big jirga held at Ladha in July 1922, at which all sections, save the Abdullais, the Jallal Khel, and the Abdur Rahman Khel, were present. In return for the new allowances identical agreements were concluded with the Shaman Khel, Alizai, and Bahlolzai in which the principles of local, sectional, and tribal responsibility were stated and their application defined; the duties of Khassadars as the sectional representatives were prescribed, and some attempt made, though inconclusively, to get Khassadars recognised by the tribe as chalweshtas and by Government as persons for whom, if killed or

---

1. Laghare means 'bare'.

killing in the execution of their duties, full blood money should always be paid by Government.

No sooner was the jirga dissolved than the Abdur Rahman Khel, who had not attended and whose special position as the recipients of an extra Rs. 6,000 per annum had not been safe-guarded, showed their resentment by an attack on a picquet near Ladha in which they killed three British soldiers and wounded three more. Having done this, they sent in word to say so and to say why they had done it. The Resident would much have liked to have seen them and the other recalcitrants dealt with by troops, but for the moment only air operations were allowed. These resulted in the so-called friendlies of the section paying the fine and producing the six rifles that had been demanded of them. The blockade against them was consequently raised. The question of their extra grant does not appear to have been raised, but they were given hopes of Government assistance in cultivating lands at Spinkai Kach in the Gumal. This left only the Abdullais and the Jallal Khel out. In November the latter were responsible for a raid in the Dera Ismail Khan District which seems to have been intended to kidnap the Chief Commissioner on tour. They failed to catch him but waylaid another motor near Yarik out of which, after shooting the driver, they kidnapped a Post Office Superintendent, an Extra Assistant Commissioner, and six other persons. The prisoners were however speedily released without ransom. About the same time the Government of India wishing to satisfy itself finally that the policy of linking up Jandola by road with Razmak and of holding the line so formed as far as Sara Rogha by Scout posts, was really sound, deputed two Members of Council to visit Waziristan and report after seeing things for themselves. This visit produced considerable excitement amongst the Mahsuds and had disturbing consequences. At the close of the year therefore, as the advance on Razmak was taking place, the troops from Ladha were once more used on punitive operations against the Abdullais of Makin, prior to the evacuation of the Takki Zam line by regulars, and air operations were undertaken against the Garrarais and Guri Khel of Ahmadwam in the Inzar Valley and other Manzai sections, and the Jallal Khel. The first named had been responsible for killing Lieutenant Dickson, R.E., in Mohmit Khel Wazir limits, as he was choosing the alignment for the road, and the others had been active in raiding and minor attacks on troops. Makin and the adjacent villages were even more effectively dealt with this time than on the previous occasion, but the opposition encountered by the troops was not serious. The Mahsuds were in fact now trying a different line of tactics. They sent a numerous deputation to Kabul which was able to persuade the authorities to take up their cause. Strong protests were accordingly made to the British Minister (Colonel Humphrys) by the Afghan Foreign Office that the recent operations, of which no previous intimation had been given to them, were in violation of Article XI of the treaty and of its appended letters. These communications were enforced by His Majesty the Amir himself by verbal argument, but neither Mahsuds nor Afghans got any change out of this manoeuvre. The protests were effectively countered and the operations both by land and air were prosecuted to a successful conclusion, though not before Major Parsons, the Political Agent, had been severely wounded while directing a bombing raid on the Jallal Khel from the air. The recalcitrant sections submitted in February 1923 and about the same time decisions were taken that the military occupation of Waziristan should be prolonged for nine months and the completion of the Sara Rogha-Razmak link and of the Jandola-Sarwakai road pressed on in earnest. In March a jirga of about 1,500 men, not wholly representative, was seen by the Force Commander at Tauda China camp, and the policy and intentions of Government were declared and accepted without protest. There still however remained a strong body of irreconcilables in the tribe and Afghan intrigue, now mainly conducted through Lala Pir from Khost, was intermittently active. These die-hards committed numerous offences in the district and made some serious attacks upon the troops in occupation. But such incidents did not prevent the road construction programme from being steadily carried out—again with the loss of a young and zealous officer of the Royal Engineers. This was Lieutenant Webster who was shot at close quarters by three Mahsuds near Piazha in July. By the end of 1923 the Takki Zam road had been very hastily completed and the Shahur road was through by May 1924.

After being wounded Major Parsons had been relieved as Political Agent by Major Thompson Glover in March 1923. The new Political Agent had served during the Great War in the Royal Air Force and it was largely owing to his initiative and energy that during this period, in the intervals of active operations, an aerial survey of Mahsud country was completed and a register made of all visible habitations, which has proved of immense value on numerous occasions. In the summer of the same year Sir John Maffey went on long leave and was succeeded as Chief Commissioner by Mr (now Sir Norman) Bolton. In May of the following year Mr Pears relinquished charge as Resident and was succeeded by Mr Howell, the author of these pages. This would obviously be a suitable point at which to bring this narrative to a close. It is, however, necessary to round off one aspect of the situation a little.

Reference has lately been frequent to the hostiles (badi-daran). This term had now acquired a special meaning. It designated not so much those who led raids or attacked the troops as those who had held aloof from the numerous settlements made in 1921–3, and had received no share in allowances or khassadari service. Those who had so held aloof were generally able to do so only because of support in some form or other—allowances, lands, or khassadari service—given them by the Afghans. These marks of favour in turn were generally reserved by the Afghans for those who had distinguished themselves by signal acts of hostility against us, and so the two meanings more or less coincided. But some hostiles did us no harm, while many so-called friendlies did all the harm they could.

It is recorded by the Chief Commissioner in his review of events in the year 1923–4 that 75 per cent of the offences committed by Mahsuds were the work of hostiles residing in Afghanistan, and it was clear that if these could be restrained, the remaining tale of crime would be insignificant. Of the numerous offences committed in that season by the hostile Abdur Rahman Khel, Jallal Khel, Faridai, Marisai, and by the Guri Khel—friendly as well as hostile sections—five were important. These took place at Chesan Kach in February, at Chagmalai and Khirgi in March, at Saggu in April, and near Manjhi in May 1924. In these affairs one British officer and twenty three Indian other ranks, regular and irregular, lost their lives, twelve Indian other ranks were wounded, three Powinda badraggas were killed, nine British subjects (Hindus) were kidnapped, one Lewis gun and twenty-one rifles, besides other miscellaneous equipment and property were taken. Only in the last of these affairs—the Manjhi raid, a daring ambush of Frontier Constabulary by a very large gang—had the forces of Government been able to get any of their own back. Several portions of the gang were intercepted on their return journey by parties of the South Waziristan Scouts, using the advantage given them by possession of the Jandola-Sarwakai line. Five or six of the raiders were killed—amongst them the notorious Ghulam Khan, Jallal Khel. Bombing operations were also sanctioned against the Abdur Rahman Khel, with whom all the Jallal Khel hostiles were living, but too late to catch them before their return to their lands in Afghanistan. How to secure reparation and bring these miscreants under control was then the main pre-occupation. A big jirga of the Bahlolzai was held at Tank in December 1924, at which the principles of full tribal responsibility were re-affirmed and accepted, but it was not possible to make this cover reparation for the past misdeeds above enumerated. Towards the close of the cold weather, sanction was obtained for air operations against the Guri Khel—hostile and friendly—and soon after, permission was given to deal in the same way with the hostiles of the other sections. A fine of thirty Government rifles was announced to cover all past offences. The terms were not complied with and on 9 March air operations began. They continued practically without intermission until 1 May, when, the last of all the recalcitrants, the Abdur Rahman Khel submitted and the whole fine—less one rifle remitted to the Biland Khel Guri Khel for good treatment of a wounded airman prisoner—was in due course recovered. The acceptance by these sections of these terms involved the return of all their hostiles into the tribal fold, without extra provision being made for them, and the consequent abolition of the technical distinction between hostile and friendly. It involved the final rejection of the Abdur Rahman Khel claim to their special grant, and it involved a redistribution within the sections of their sectional shares of allowances and khassadari. This in turn of course meant a reduction to all previous recipients. Nevertheless it was all in due course effected.

Since the conclusion of this little campaign, the first to be carried through by the Royal Air Force entirely by themselves, the tale of Mahsud crime has been negligible and with one trifling exception in 1928, when aeroplanes were employed against the Nekzan and Giga Khel, no further operations of any kind against any part of the tribe have been necessary until the disturbances of 1930.

Chapter X

Well and what is the moral of all this long story? When the manuscript of this monograph was about two thirds completed, I lent it to an officer of the Department, one already marked by distinction, to read. In due course he handed it back to me and said 'What a record of futility it all is!' The criticism is certainly pungent, but perhaps not penetrating. Not all the men who have handled Mahsud affairs in the past can be set down as fools. Macaulay indeed and some of his successors were very much the contrary, and if, after eighty years or so, the Mahsud problem still remains without a final solution, we must, instead of condemning those who went before us, concede that it may have been so difficult as to be perhaps insoluble, anyhow with the means at their disposal.

What then were the difficulties? First, subjugation by passing 'the military steam roller over the country from end to end'—to quote Lord Curzon's phrase—has so far proved, if not absolutely beyond the power of the Government of India, at least relatively beyond the degree of strength which they were at any given moment prepared to exert and to continue exerting for the requisite period. This perhaps explains why his Lordship was reluctant to start that machine. The military critic who has seen the British bull dog emerge from the mud of Flanders with the Prussian eagle strangled in his jaws may snort with indignation at any such contention. But in point of fact has it not been so and is it not still so? Whether it is the proximity of sanctuary in Afghanistan or the difficult nature of his country and its lack of resources or his own strong right arm and virile qualities which have so far preserved the Mahsud from subjugation, or the combination of all these causes, the fact remains, that he has not yet come under the yoke. The Mahsud has not yet been disarmed. His country is not administered and he pays no taxes. On the contrary he is better armed than he has ever been before. He receives handsome allowances and immense sums for khassadar service. For the regulation of his private affairs he follows no law save his own queer crooked notions of honour and his grim rule of reprisals. There can be no doubt of it. The nut has so far proved too hard for the crackers. So when the soldier impatiently inveighs against the defects of the Political Department, with its endless jirgas and its immoral money bags, it is sometimes tempting, though perhaps not tactful, to remind him of this very essential factor in the situation.

The Mahsud being still unsubjugated, it falls next to consider the other reasons which make him no less difficult to deal with on planes other than that of force than he is to conquer in the field. First, there are the same qualities which make him formidable as a fighter—his ingenuity and his persistence, backed by amazing plausibility in argument, such as would excite the envy of an Athenian demagogue. Next—and it is remarkable that this quality should be combined alike with discipline in the field and with the strong feeling which lies behind the tribal sarishta—there is that complex of mental attributes which results or may at any time result in utter recklessness of the consequences of individual action and consequent complete lack of tribal cohesion. The famous Jaggar, Abdur Rahman Khel, once said to me 'Let it be "field"[1] and blow us all up with cannon, or make all eighteen thousand[2] of us Nawabs'. What he had in mind was the *liberum veto* which any young hot head could exercise by the use of his rifle, as has indeed so often and so disastrously happened.

Reference was made above to the tribal sarishta—the immutable or slowly changing law which fixes the share of each section in all tribal loss and gain. We have seen how from the earliest times our officers— Graham, Macaulay, Bruce, Merk, Johnston, and others—have come up against this and fallen back defeated. No matter how the political officer of the time has wished or tried to make what he regarded as a proper distribution of the benefits in his gift, in the end he has always been forced to conform more or less closely to the tribal notion. So merit has often gone unrewarded, while iniquity has prospered.

Constant intrigue in Mahsud affairs by successive rulers of Afghanistan is another adverse factor to which almost every page of our narrative bears witness. Far less apparent, but perhaps more powerful is the institution of the blood feud, which operates in a number of ways. Its unseen retarding

---

1. Good Mahsud Pashto for 'active service'.
2. The traditional number of Mahsud fighting men. I reckon it to be about two-thirds of the right number at present.

influence is perhaps of these the most potent. Indeed I believe this to be the root cause of the economic difficulty, which is the bane of the whole tribal belt. No man whose hold on life is as insecure as that of the average tribesman, whether Mahsud, Afridi, or what you will, can readily command capital; nor if at any time a sum of money comes into his hand can he lay it out on such things as water-courses, orchards, or improvements to the land of any kind. He is compelled to spend it on weapons, whether of defence, such as towers and kots, or of offence, such as the latest pattern of military rifle. The retarding influence does not stop at that. It is also a powerful check not only on individual initiative but on all forms of collective enterprise. Nothing is more remarkable throughout Waziristan—and I believe the same to be true of Tirah—than the traces of terraced fields which remain to show that once men grew corn where now there is no tillage. In Waziristan anyhow local tradition is unanimous that it was in the days of the Marwats or the Urmars that, these lands were cultivated and mainly all the water channels of any size or length which still survive were cut. What is it if not the blood feud— and the temper from which the blood feud springs—which has kept the active, intelligent, and—till we spoilt him—industrious Mahsud, whose coming is comparatively recent, from turning his land to as good account as did its former occupants? But the blood feud works also in other ways nearer the surface than this. In times past the chalweshta may have been a visible embodiment of the tribal will and a sacrosanct executor of its fiat. But even Macaulay found that he could not create chalweshtas for the purposes of Government and in their absence the fear of vengeance at the hands of fellow tribesmen has sufficed to make any form of tribal police or any attempt to exercise effective control through maliks very barren of results. Government could pay but not protect, and there has thus been a constant tendency for the rewards of service, which should only be earned by service, to slide into the booty of the stronger which can be extorted from fear or a too ready complaisance. Lastly, though the Mahsud is not fanatical as the Daur and the Bannuchi are fanatical, he is sufficiently so to put a halo round the heads of all those who have been prominent in opposition to the Sirkar, whatever form their opposition may have taken.

All these are causes operating from the Mahsud side, but factors operating amongst ourselves have also to be taken into account. A transborder agency is a charge which imposes upon the holder a heavy strain, physical, mental, and, we may perhaps add, moral. It is not every officer, even amongst members of a picked corps, who is fit or by temperament apt to carry the burden, and even amongst the few who are there are fewer still who can stand the strain for long at a time. Consequently changes of incumbency are of necessity frequent, and Government are for ever being compelled to change their tools just as these are becoming shaped to their task. This drawback, with its inevitable consequences, dislocation, and lack of continuity, is inseparable from the common measure of human infirmity and gives Government no more valid ground of complaint against their officers than that they are not all supermen. The local officers on the other hand may perhaps have more legitimate cause of complaint against Government—and here we may perhaps be reminded of the dictum with which this chapter began. They might urge with some show of reason that the policy of Government has often, perhaps more often than not, lacked definition. For the first thirty years Government can scarcely be said to have had any policy other than that of holding the Mahsud at arm's length. In this period with very little encouragement or support and less guidance, working so to speak with nothing but his bare hands, Major Macaulay during his long tenure showed how much against all odds a great personality could achieve. If Macaulay had been given the same scope as Sandeman the Waziristan problem might have been solved as the Balushistan problem was solved. But Macaulay came too late. The second Afghan War coincided with the last three years of his term, and though the events which preceded and accompanied that war no doubt brought clearly to light the disadvantages of the political vacuum which it had been his duty to maintain, the necessity for avoiding diffusion of energy in war time precluded all attempts at the initiation of a more fruitful policy. This then was thus reserved for Mr Bruce who arrived on the scene six years after Macaulay's departure bringing with him the Sandeman outfit from Baluchistan. Had he been allowed or perhaps, one might more correctly say, had it in fact been possible for him to apply the Sandeman policy in its entirety to Waziristan, all might still have been well. But, as we have seen, penetration, which is the essence of the Sandeman scheme was ruled out almost from the start. I do not say that it was not in the circumstances rightly ruled out. For in the absence of a Sandeman or a Macaulay penetration of Mahsud country, as we have since learnt, must have meant large concentrations of troops, the construction of roads, and vast expenditure. But without penetration the rest of the Sandeman outfit is mere junk. 'Let there be maliks', said Mr Bruce and there were maliks. But without support from within what could they do? They could, as we have seen, on one occasion, procure the surrender of five important malefactors, but only at the cost of their own lives, and natrually their example has since found few imitators. Without penetration and protection for those who served Government loyally, Mr Bruce's system could lead nowhere and did lead nowhere except into the morass from which Mr Merk sought to find an escape by throwing the maliks overboard and substituting for their inefficiency his utterly impracticable plan of dealing only with the 'great jirga of the Mahsuds', which perished still born.

'It hath been the wisdom of the Church of England, ever since the first compiling of her public liturgy, to keep the mean between the two extremes of too much stiffness in refusing and too much easiness in admitting any variation from it.' The Government of India never compiled any liturgy to be observed by frontier politicals, and, if they had, no such boast could sit upon their lips. In the creation of maliks by Mr Bruce, the destruction of maliks by Mr Merk, and their re-creation by Mr Johnston, we see Government swing with all too great facility from one extreme to the opposite. Nor were they content only to let their local officers lead them. Upon occasions they have played an active role. After the maliks had been re-created by Mr Johnston, it was they who insisted upon taking under their wing that first class scoundrel, Mulla Powinda, and they who sanctioned a gift of land for him, in order to undermine his influence, just at the very same moment when the list of those maliks who were to receive stipends from Government was put into his hands for revision! Is it surprising that in the midst of these oscillations the growth of an oligarchy attached to Government by material ties should not have prospered? Other momentous changes there have been—the withdrawal of the regulars in 1904; the creation of the militias; the elimination, restoration, and second elimination of the Mahsud element in those militias; the introduction of the khassadar. But the issues raised by these—except the last—are now dead and as for the khassadar and the question whether he is the *deus ex machina* or a Frankenstein monster, I do not propose to express an opinion. I have no wish to tread—'*per ignes suppositos cineri doloso*'.

Of the men in authority at headquarters, whether in the Punjab Government or the Government of India, it is not necessary to say more than that if they had not had remarkable qualities they would presumably not have been chosen for the high offices which they held. Their secretariats too have been manned by selected officers of a high standard of ability, and, as we have said before, the local officers have also as a rule been picked men. How is it then that the blunders which we have indicated were not avoided? The causes which suggest themselves are the lack of leisure in high places, the lack of a proper liaison between the local officers and headquarters, and the lack of expert knowledge in the secretariat. If these seem insufficient, let it be reflected how great a diversion of the ship follows from a slight deflection of the rudder. The moral seems to be clear. Changes in policy should be accepted only with the greatest caution. Proposals must be examined with meticulous care and their ulterior as well as their immediate effects carefully considered. Anything which runs counter to well-established psychological principles, such as that unearned money means demoralisation, is bound to do more harm than good in the end and should be rejected. It is easier to take a bone from a savage dog than to discontinue any form of financial assistance once sanctioned to the Mahsud. It is not suggested therefore that existing allowances should be cancelled by a stroke of the pen, but rather that the objects for which they are given should be carefully examined, and that Government should be chary of sanctioning any increase or of entertaining any more khassadars, and should see to it that those who are in receipt of benefit in either or both of these forms do something for their money. The amount which they may be reasonably expected to do can be gradually increased as other forms of control develop.

Finally—and here we move from the past to the future—it is not now too soon to consider the goal. To keep the Mahsud from raiding in British India is a considerable achievement, but cannot be a final end of policy. What is the final end? Possibilities, so far as can be foreseen, are three. The old welter may continue, or Mahsud country may become part of Afghanistan and the Mahsuds throw in his lot with the inhabitants of that country, or he must be trained to take his place in the federation of India. To that, as to Tipperary, is a long long way to go, but it is the only one of the three to which our officers can worthily address themselves.

NOTES

NOTE NO. 1

Herbert Edwardes in his book *A year in the Punjab*, Vol. I, page 248 mentions four Mahsud maliks as 'chiefs of note' thus:

'As this is the last mention I shall probably have to make of these remote Vizeerees, I may as well append the following memorandum:

| The Vizeerees of | Muhsood, or Muksood, or Musjeet, | have 4 chiefs of note: | Nusrattee *(a)* Jungee Khan *(b)* Sidh *(c)* Golanee *(d)*'. |

(a) Nusrattee was an Abdullai, see Appendix II.
(b) For Jungee Khan see Appendix II.
(c) Probably meant for Sadhi, Langar Khel, and not Sidh, Abdullai.
(d) Golanee, Nazar Khel, was father of Shadi Khan, second class malik in Mr Bruce's list of 1895. Shadi Khan was father of Muhammad Ali Khan, now a malik of Rs. 15 p.m.

NOTE NO. 2

MacGregor in his *Central Asia* writes 'The Mahsuds have been celebrated as the earliest, the most inveterate, and the most incorrigible of all the robbers of the border. It is not possible, in the state of district records, to get a really accurate list of their offences against British territory from the beginning, but I have extracted such as are recorded from the year 1853 to 1860.'

For statistics of Mahsud crime from 1853 to 1926 see Appendix I.

NOTE NO. 3

(Facsimile reproduction of list of 1923)

Names of the horsemen of the Mahsud Waziri tribes selected (in 1865) for service under the British Government

ALIZAIS

*M. Syad Makhmad Khan, son of Jangi Khan, Suleman Khel *(a)*.
   Muhammad Afzal Khan, son of M. Yarak Khan, Langar Khel.
   Mir Khan, son of M. Sarfaraz Khan, Michi Khel *(b)*.
M. Surdee Khan[1] Bahadur Khel.
   Uzmat Khan, Kahi Khel *(c)*.
   Khummai Khan, Shahabi Khel *(d)*.
   Pajuk Khan, Shahabi Khel.
M. Kajul Khan, Gooree Khel.

SHAMAN KHEL

M. Khanzum Khan[2] Zariya Khel.
   Lal Shah Khan *(e)*.
M. Mummiodin Khan, Badowai *(f)*.
M. Syad Amin Khan, Galeshai *(g)*.
   Nur Khan *(h)*.
   Naseer Khan,[3] son of M. Pir Gul Khan, Sarumshahi Kasim Khel.
   Didun Khan *(i)*.
   Surmast Khan,[4] Haiduaoi, Kashim Khel of Shahur *(j)*.

BAHLOLZAI (AMAL KHEL)

M. Fatteh Khan, Malikshahi.
   Suddurmak Khan, Nazar Khel.
M. Niazi Khan, Abdullai.

SHINGI

   Billand Khan, Mummiya Khel.
   Libas Khan, Khurmuj Khel.
   Shah Alam Khan, nephew of M. Jana Khan, Boee Khel.
This list is described by Mr Bruce as 'particularly reliable'. It contains
22 names—8 Alizai, 8 Shaman Khel, and 6 Bahlolzai, of whom none were
Nana Khel. Apparently that section had not decided who their representatives
were to be.

The genealogical trees of some of these 22 horsemen, showing the present
representatives of their families, will be found in Appendix II.

---

*   M stands for Malik.
1. Haji Muhammad Khan in his place.
2. In his place Sahib Khan.
3. Nazeem Khan in his place.
4. Mummodin Khan in his place.

Notes on others are attached.

(a) Suleman Khel for Salimi Khel.

(b) *Ex*-Subedar Hayat Khan (Rs. 130) is of a different family.

(c) Batakai really.

(d) Grand-father of Matadin (Rs. 25) Astonai.

(e) Father of Balak (Rs. 30), Chahar Khel.

(f) Father of K. S. Marwat (Rs. 130), Kahi Khel.

(g) Father of Ali Khan[1] -father of Suhail (Rs. 75) Galishai.

(h) Galishai, but lived with Badiwai.

(i) Badiwai.

(j) Haidaoi for Haidarai.

Those not noted upon above have no modern representatives of mark.

NOTE NO. 4

Letter from Major Graham, Deputy Commissioner, Dera Ismail Khan, to the Commissioner, Derajat Division

'Though I am convinced of the sound policy of treating the three sections in this negotiation with equal consideration, still I am aware that it is almost a necessity to increase the Shingi and perhaps the Nana Khel horsemen, if it is hoped to restrain these sub-divisions from returning to their old practices. In fact I regard the persistent refusal of the Shingis to come to terms as a very good proof of their consciousness that they would hereafter have to depend on the means of subsistence provided by Government as a substitute for plunder. I have therefore determined to take the opportunity of vacancies occurring in the Frontier Horse Militia and District Mounted Police gradually to provide for a few more of them; and to enable me to do this the more effectually I beg the support of yourself and of the Brigadier-General Commanding the Punjab Frontier Force in allowing me to have the first vacancies in the three districts of the Division to the extent of ten places, to be hereafter recovered from this district.'

NOTE NO. 5

This preference was rudely shaken by Nabi Khan's omission to warn Major Macaulay of Umar Khan's preparations to raid Tank, an omission which is difficult to explain, since the attack on Tank was really a move in Mahsud party

---

1. Abdul Ghafur was killed in 1887 at the instigation of Umar Khan—R. I. BRUCE.

politics directed against Nabi Khan's own faction and position. After the raid
Nabi Khan fell rapidly. In 1880 he was convicted of systematic receiving of
stolen property. He was sentenced to two years' imprisonment and died shortly
after his release.

NOTE NO. 6

It was during the summer of 1888 that Umar Khan met his end.
Mr Bruce writes:

'Since writing this memorandum Umar Khan, the leading Mahsud Malik,
has been killed by his nephews, Azammi and Haji, in revenge for the death of
Haji's brother, Abdul Ghafur.[1] His son, Badshah Khan, has been elected in his
stead. Although Umar Khan's life was taken in prosecution of the blood feud,
still at the time he was killed he was actually engaged in trying to recover some
Government arms and other property which had been stolen from the military
post at Manjhi and had got into Azammi's possession. After Umar Khan's death
these arms were restored to me through the instrumentality of Badshah Khan
and certain other Maliks.'

(Sd.) R. I. BRUCE,
Deputy Commissioner, Dera Ismail Khan.

November 1888.

NOTE NO. 7

Translation of a petition presented by the Mahsud Maliks to R. I. Bruce, Esq.,
C.I.E., Deputy Commissioner, at Appozai on 19 January 1890

We most respectfully beg to represent that on being summoned by the
Government (Sarkar) we, all the Maliks of each of the three sections of the
Mahsuds, have presented ourselves at Appozai. Your honour has informed us that
the Government intends to pacify the Gomal Pass and establish communication
through it with Zhob and elsewhere, and for ensuring the safety of these routes
and maintaining peace in the country, proposes to grant us pay and allowances
and entertain us in their service. We are greatly pleased with this arrangement
and willingly accept the pay and allowances Government has graciously been
pleased to fix for our tribe, in return for which we in future hold ourselves
responsible for the safety and protection of the road, and will cheerfully comply

---

1. Abdul Ghafur was killed in 1887 at the instigation of Umar Khan—R. I. BRUCE.

with any orders that the Government may be pleased to give, and will always remain united to and on friendly terms with the Sarkar. We have distributed among ourselves the amount Government has been pleased to fix for service by common consent and according to tribal usage.

We trust that in future Government will regard us as their own subjects and treat us with kindness, and we Maliks and our nominees, levies, will always be present when required and ready to do the Government service. In whatever places Government may be pleased to fix posts for our nominees, levies, they will remain there without objections and serve the Government faithfully.

ALIZAIS (25)

Badshah Khan	Zamin Khan
Mirbaz Khan	Imam Shah
Shah Salim	Tor Khan
Zebae	Shahbaz Khan
Badrodin	Nilgar Khan
Jana Khan	Nasar Khan, son of Mandi
Nazar Shah	Mustafa Khan
Azmat Khan	Dinak
Tersam Khan	Kaisar Khan
Mir Azam	Shahzor Khan
Khudrae	Abbat Khan
Zalla Khan	Said Amin
Shahawal Khan	

BAHLOLZAIS (35)

Awalli Shah	Byak Khan
Ismail	Amir Khan
Kajir	Azim Khan
Futteh Khan	Zobar Khan
Muhammad Ali Khan	Muhammad
Jang Bahadur	Ashik Khan
Rahimdad Khan	Mir Ajal
Gulpir Khan	Kargal Khan
Abozai Khan	Muhammad Afzal
Nazir Khan	Dawagar Khan
Tala Khan	Laisar Khan
Ghazal Khan	Maisar Khan
Mamak Khan	Jambil Khan

Sanjar Khan   Karam Khan
Salehin   Kaisar Khan
Muhammad Ashraf Khan   Gulzar Khan, son of Bashak
Baramat Khan   Khalwat Khan
                Mingai Khan

SHAMAN KHELS (29)

Mitha Khan   Fakir
Nazim Khan   Chehat Khan
Ghazi Khan   Nur Shah
Nasir Khan   Fatteh Mir Khan
Allah Bagh   Ahyun
Haji Muhammad Khan   Zarpayao
Khadim Khan   Ila Khan
Said Amin   Bilak, son of Lal Shah
Parang   Karman Khan
Fatteh Roz   Lal Gul
Badraka Khan   Gulzar
Alijan   Etil Khan
Kohistan   Pulad
Mir Akbar Khan   Azad Khan
                Ism Shah

NOTE NO. 8

The three men killed were:

(1) Karim Khan, Nazar Khel. He appears as a malik of the 5th class in Mr Bruce's list of 1895.

(2) Chaprai, son of Arsala, Abdullai. His brother Azim Khan appears as a malik of the 1st class in Mr Bruce's list of 1895.

(3) Dawagar, Giga Khel. His name is not in the 1895 list, but that of his son M. Afzal is. He is entered as a malik of the 2nd class.

The men expelled were:

(1) Mir Ajal, Haibat Khel. He appears as a malik of the 1st class in Mr Bruce's list of 1895.

(2) Bramat, Nazar Khel, the father of Hayat and *ex*-Subedar Baloch Khan. He too appears as a malik of the 1st class in the 1895 list.

Note No. 9

This ultimately moved to Sarwakai, for the retention of a military force at which place the special sanction of the Secretary of State was obtained in 1895.

Note No. 10

A copy of this list is on record at Proceeding No. 106-A., in Proceedings Secret, F, August 1895, Nos. 106–118. All local officers concerned have received copies of it.

What exactly maliks of each class received is not stated. There were 270 maliks in all and, so far as can be calculated, the rates of stipend were:

	Per mensem
First Class	Rs. 30
Second Class	15
Third Class	10
Fourth Class	5
Fifth Class	3

Note No. 11

Nine maliks in receipt of allowances from the British Government went with Mulla Powinda to Kabul. These were:
(Proceedings Frontier A., May 1897, Nos. 28–59, No. 52)—

Alizai—
　Azam, Guri Khel.
　Shahnir, Shabi Khel.
Bahlolzai—
　Daraz Khan, Nekzan Khel.
　Muhammad Afzal Nekzan Khel.
　Malang, Haibat Khel.
　Sheikh Amir (*alias* Mamakki), Umar Khel.
　Khwaja Baz, Umar Khel.
　Saleh Din, Malikshahi.
　Salihin Shingi.

All of these were in Mr Bruce's list of 1895. Azam, Shahnir, Khwaja Baz, Saleh Din, and Salihin were in the fourth class, the rest were in the third. Their allowances were forfeited for eight months and then restored.

NOTE NO. 12

A specimen of the Mulla's correspondence may be of interest. It was sent on 11 March 1897, was addressed to the Assistant District Superintendent of Police and the Political Officer, and runs as follows:

'It is known to the Deputy Commissioner and to Ghulam Muhammad Khan that when I went to Kabul I made a petition to the Amir to the effect that we did not wish to give our country to the English, and that if they had come and taken possession of it, they should buy it.

The Amir of Islam sent our petition to the Viceroy of India, and wrote that the English should either leave the country or purchase it.

Our petition was an humble request to the Amir.

The Viceroy replied that he would not take forcible possession of the country.

Now you are commencing to build. If these buildings are completed, the Mussalmans will suffer injury, and you will lose bahaduri.'

No doubt it correctly represents the author's own impression of what passed between himself, the Amir, and Government. Mulla Powinda was himself illiterate. His secretary at this time was Mulla Hamzullah who died in 1924.

NOTE NO. 13

In February 1899 a gang of Shingis raided Suleman Khal flocks near Kot Nasran, carried off 1,200 heads of sheep and goats, and killed five of the Suleman Khel pursuit party. Mr Anderson happened to be in camp near Nasran. He took prompt action. Troops from Jandola rounded up the Shingi villages between there and Kotkai and a general barampta of Shingis throughout the Dera Ismail Khan District was made. Prompt redress for the Suleman Khel was thus secured. All compensation due was paid and twelve of the ring-leaders of the gang were surrendered for trial and sentenced to terms of imprisonment varying from three to five years.

NOTE NO. 14

Between April and July 1900, 53 offences by Mahsuds against British subjects and 9 against persons other than British subjects were recorded. Of the former 26 were committed in British India. The total bill on account of these amounted to a little less than Rs. 27,000.

NOTE NO. 15

Agreement by the Mahsud jirga, dated 5 April 1902

Government has been pleased to grant allowances to the Mahsud tribe.

Therefore, in consideration of these allowances, we, the full tribal jirga; completely representing the whole Mahsud tribe, hereby bind the whole tribe to faithfully abide by the following conditions, for compelling the observance of which, we, the tribal jirga, are responsible; we, the Mahsud tribe, will be loyal to Government; we will be of good conduct and commit no offences in areas occupied by Government, that is to say districts like Bannu, Dera Ismail Khan, the Sherani country, or Wana or the Tochi, or roads like the Gomal or other trade routes; or against Government interests in any way; it is the duty of the tribe to control and keep in order all and every member of our tribe, and all the Mahsuds are jointly responsible for every Mahsud without exception within our limits and for any others who reside in our country; this responsibility is full joint tribe or sectional responsibility as Government chooses, coupled, if Government pleases, with the punishment of individual offenders; we will not give passage to any persons committing offences; we will not harbour any outlaws from any areas occupied by Government but will immediately expel them should they reach us. We will promptly settle all cases considered established against us, and should we fail to promptly give satisfaction and reparation as required by Government, it is open to Government to enforce our responsibility and obtain satisfaction and redress in any way it pleases whatever. If we fail to observe, or if we break, any of the above conditions, Government may act as it pleases and punish us as it thinks fit.

2. The distribution of the allowances has been unanimously settled in jirga as follows:

The Alizai, Bahlolzai, and Shaman Khel shares are equal, *viz.*, one-third each of Rs. 54,000. But the Shaman Khels have paid towards the fine a considerably less amount than the other divisions; of this sum the Alizai and Bahlolzai have remitted Rs. 2,500. The balance, about Rs. 5,500, the Shaman Khels will repay to the Alizai and Bahlolzai in two equal instalments. The internal distribution of sectional shares is as in the separate paper attached (Appendix A). Here follow 144 seals and 1,421 names of Mahsuds who have no seals and have made their marks.

Note No. 16

Jaggar, Abdur Rahman Khel, was one of the hostages surrendered after the campaign of 1894–5. Jaggar was believed to have been concerned in the murder of Mr Kelly in 1893 and in the subsequent killing of the maliks through whom the surrender of some of the other murderers for trial was effected. He led the attack on the camp at Wana in November 1894 and was wounded but recovered. While detained as a hostage in Dera Ismail Khan he broke out one night and was arrested bearing arms. For this he was sentenced to four years' rigorous imprisonment, in spite of the Mulla's intercession on his behalf. On release after having served his term he went back to Mahsud country and once more became prominent in raiding. I knew him well in 1906. On one occasion he told me a story out of Sa'adi's Gulistan (Bk. I, No. 16) in illustration of his own affairs. When he joined Mianji he was also given a large grant of land at Ghosba. Jaggar died in Afghanistan. His son Amir Khan has never returned to Mahsud country.

Appendix I

CRIMES COMMITTED IN THE TANK VALLEY (1853–60)						
Year	**Murder** Section 302	**Dacoity** Section 394–397	**Robbery** Section 392	**House-breaking** Section 457	**Other Petty Offences**	**Total Number of Offences**	**Remarks**
1853		1	–	–	–	1	The IPC was not yet in force and the abstract has been prepared from MacGregor's narrative (Central Asia, Part I, Vol. II, pp. 310–5). E. B. Howell,–1.9.26
1854	1	2	–	–	–	3	
1855	1	7	–	–	–	8	
1856	3	23	1	–	–	27	
1857	6	31	–	3	–	40	
1858	5	37	2	1	3	48	
1859–60	–	13	–	–	–	13	
Total	16	114	3	4	3	140	

CRIMES COMMITTED IN THE TANK VALLEY (1861–70)						
Year	**Murder** Section 302	**Dacoity** Section 394–397	**Robbery** Section 392	**House-breaking** Section 457	**Other Petty Offences**	**Total Number of Offences**	**Remarks**
1861	–	15	2	6	83	106	In these ten years the tribe made no redress for the crimes committed in British territory. C. E. Macaulay, Major Deputy Commissioner (1872–81)
1862	–	16	2	7	49	74	
1863	1	17	13	12	52	95	
1864	1	40	7	15	64	127	
1865	2	22	14	22	88	148	
1866	1	5	13	18	68	105	
1867	4	9	10	26	77	126	
1868	1	17	7	35	81	141	
1869	4	15	15	21	81	136	
1870	2	28	15	15	78	138	
Total	16	184	98	177	721	1,196	

CRIMES COMMITTED IN THE TANK VALLEY (1871–80)*

Year	Murder (Section 302)	Kidnapping (Section 363)	Grievous Hurt (Section 226)	Dacoity	Robbery	House-breaking (Section 457)	Other Petty Offences	Total	Value of property stolen			Redress Obtained			Balance			Remarks
									Rs.	a.	p.	Rs.	a.	p.	Rs.	a.	p.	
1871	4	1	2	30	14	10	47	108	14,065	15	6	6,528	8	0	7,537	7	6	Nominal as it is unrecoverable.
1872	-	2	1	22	18	9	26	78	7,997	1	6	1,852	9	0	6,144	8	6	Do.
1873	2	-	-	13	7	11	35	68	6,846	10	6	6,005	6	6	841	3	0	Do.
1874	-	2	-	7	2	1	5	17	2,153	7	0	2,008	2	0	145	4	0	Do.
1875	1	1	-	1	3	3	11	20	3,702	11	0	3,531	10	0	171	1	0	Not traced anywhere.
1876	6	1	1	3	3	3	10	27	3,138	12	0	3,138	12	0	-	-	-	
1877	1	1	4	1	2	8	14	31	1,258	13	0	1,258	13	0	-	-	-	
1878	1	-	-	-	-	4	4	9	211	5	9	211	5	9	-	-	-	
1879	3	-	-	14	3	7	14	41	90,581	12	0	20,124	14	0	70,456	14	0	Contains four raids in force involving loss of Rs. 66,131–10–0.
1880	2	-	-	3	5	7	19	37	4,116	13	0	3,146	0	0	859	13	0	Rs. 111–0–0 has not been included in the balance as the complainants were themselves to blame.
Total	20	8	8	94	57	63	185	436†	1,34,073	5	3	47,806	0	3	86,156	5	0	

* This sum will be recovered from the tribe who have agreed to pay one-fourth of their convoys towards its liquidation.

† The number of crimes during the last 10 years has decreased 64 per cent, as compared with the previous 10 years.

C. R. MACAULAY, Major,
Deputy Commissioner.

	OFFENCES COMMITTED BY MAHSUDS IN THE DERA ISMAIL KHAN DISTRICT						
Years	Total No. of Offences	Murders	Persons Wounded	Persons Kid-napped	Offences against Property	Recoveries	Remarks (Taken from contemporary reports)
1881–2	-	-	No statistics	-	-	-	No separate details for Mahsuds. The amount of property involved was small.
1882–3	41	-	Details not on record		-	-	
1883–4	-	-	Details not on record		-	-	
1884–5	25	-	-	-	1	1	Chiefly theft and burglary.
1885–6	52	-	Details not on record		-	-	Offences committed by individual marauders.
1886–7	30	-	Details not on record				
1887–8	44	-	Details not on record		-	-	Figures not as accurate as several offences committed during the preparations for Gomal Survey Expedition could not be recorded.
1888–9	28	1	Further details not on record		-	-	
1889–90	31	1	Further details not on record		-	-	A good number of petty offences due to the jealousy in connection with the distribution of the new servica pay and allowance.
1890–1	47	-	Details not on record		-	-	Ditto
1891–2	30	-	Details not on record		-	-	
1892–3	46	-	Details not on record		-	-	
1893–4	-	2	Further details not on record		-	-	Though some very heinous offences were committed by individual Mahsuds or sub-sections of the tribe, there was no increase in the number of offences committed by them.
1894–5	46	-	Details not on record		-	-	
1896–8	-	-	No statistics	-	-	-	
1899–1900	9	12	3	-	3	-	Besides these offences several dacoities were committed accompanied by grievous hurt.
1901–2	83	2	-	-	70	No details	
1902–3	-	-	No statistics		-	-	
1906–7	1	-	-	-	1	-	Compensation recovered.
1907–8	2	-	1	3	2	-	Compensation recovered in one case.
1908–9	6	13	1	-	4	-	Compensation recovered in two cases.
1909–10	24	8	16	6	21	7	Compensation recovered in twelve cases.
1910–11	5	-	-	2	5	4+1	Part recovery in one case.
1911–12	9	4	3	-	8	6	Compensation recovered in three cases.
1912–13	12	5	3	8	9	6	Compensation recovered in two cases.
1913–14	11	4	2	5	6	2	Compensation recovered in two cases.
1914–15	36	22	27	30	29	4+5	Compensation recovered in one case. Also 5 part recoveries.
1915–16	126	31	40	68	99	28+13	Compensation recovered in two cases. Also 13 part recoveries.
1916–17	74	31	16	111	57	24+6	Six part recoveries.
1917–18	54	41	34	26	46	9+4	Four part recoveries.
1918–19	27	3	5	16	26	3+2	Two part recoveries.
1919–20	198	99	153	127	No details		No separate details for Mahsuds.
1920–1	84	85	85	36	No details		No separate details for Mahsuds.
1921–2	51	25	30	17	No details		Ditto
1922–3	49	21	29	33	No details		Ditto
1923–4	35	19	16	6	No details		Ditto
1924–5	22	6	2	16	No details		Ditto
1925–6	6	6	5	-	No details		Ditto

Appendix II

SOME MAHSUD GENEALOGICAL TREES
Shaman Khel, Khalli Khel, Badiwai, Mir Gul Khel

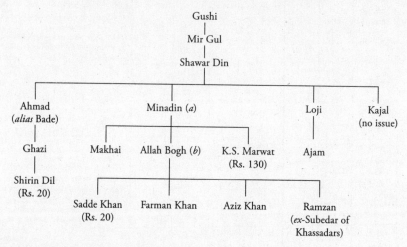

(*a*) In the list of 1865.

(*b*) In Mr Bruce's list of 1895 as a first class Malik.

Allah Bogh and Ghazi were killed by a cousin named Shah Murad in his own house whither they had gone to condole with him on the death of his son.

* * * * * * * *

Shaman Khel, Chahar Khel, Qasim Khel, Ghazi Khel, Khan Khel

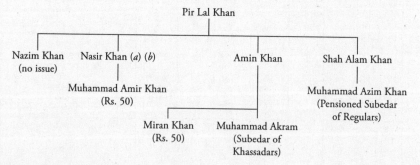

(*a*) In the list of 1865.

(*b*) In Mr Bruce's list of 1895 as a first class Malik.

Shaman Khel, Galishai, Dati Khel, Mangi Khel

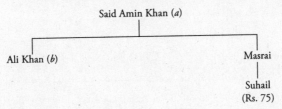

Said Amin Khan (*a*)

Ali Khan (*b*)   Masrai

Suhail
(Rs. 75)

(*a*) In the list of 1865.
(*b*) In Mr Bruce's list of 1895 as a first class Malik.

* * * * * * * *

Alizai, Manzai, Giddi Khel, Langar Khel, Nikarrab Khel, Umar Khel

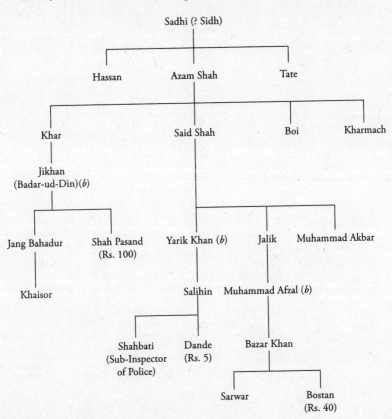

Sadhi (? Sidh)

Hassan   Azam Shah   Tate

Khar   Said Shah   Boi   Kharmach

Jikhan
(Badar-ud-Din)(*b*)

Jang Bahadur   Shah Pasand   Yarik Khan (*b*)   Jalik   Muhammad Akbar
(Rs. 100)

Khaisor   Salihin   Muhammad Afzal (*b*)

Shahbati   Dande   Bazar Khan
(Sub-Inspector   (Rs. 5)
of Police)

Sarwar   Bostan
(Rs. 40)

(*b*) In Mr Bruce's list of 1895 as a first class Malik.

Alizai, Manzai, Palli Khel, Dachi Khel, Salimi Khel

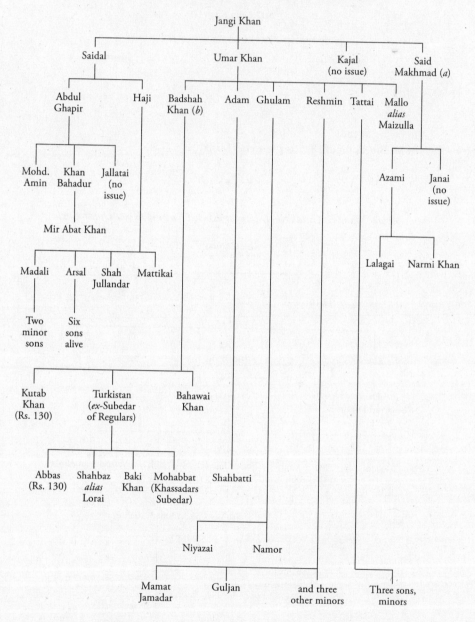

(a) In the list of 1865.

(b) In Mr Bruce's list of 1895 as a first class Malik.

Alizai, Manzai, Palli Khel, Dachi Khel, Mal Khel, Hashim Khel

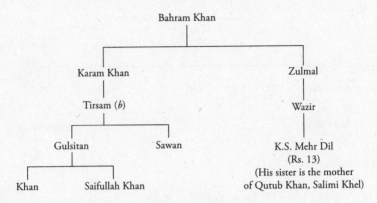

(*b*) In Mr Bruce's list of 1895 as a third class Malik.

* * * * * * * *

Alizai, Manzai, Palli Khel, Shunni Khel, Michi Khel

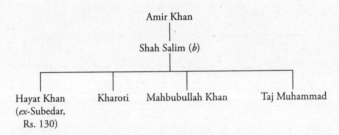

(*b*) In Mr Bruce's list of 1895 as a first class Malik.

* * * * * * * *

Bahlolzai, Nana Khel, Abdur Rahman Khel

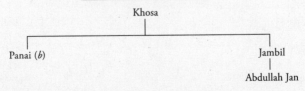

(*b*) In Mr Bruce's list of 1895 as a fourth class Malik.

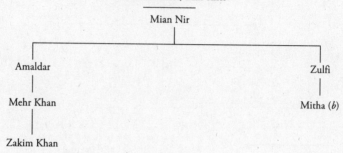

Bahlolzai, Nana Khel, Abdur Rahman Khel

Rahimdad Khel, Lalli Khel

Mian Nir

Amaldar — Zulfi

Mehr Khan — Mitha (*b*)

Zakim Khan

(*b*) In Mr Bruce's list of 1895 as a fourth class Malik.

* * * * * * * *

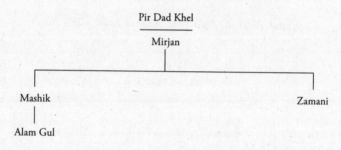

Bahlolzai, Nana Khel, Abdur Rahman Khel

Pir Dad Khel

Mirjan

Mashik — Zamani

Alam Gul

* * * * * * * *

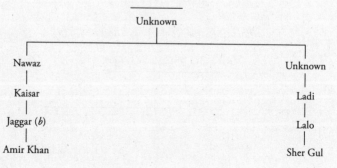

Bahlolzai, Nana Khel, Abdur Rahman Khel

Pir Dad Khel, Nazi Khel

Unknown

Nawaz — Unknown

Kaisar — Ladi

Jaggar (*b*) — Lalo

Amir Khan — Sher Gul

(*b*) In Mr Bruce's list of 1895 as a third class Malik.

Bahlolzai, Aimal Khel, Abdullai, Shamak Khel, Azdi Khel

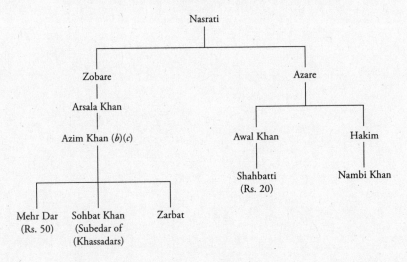

(*b*) In Mr Bruce's list of 1895 as a first class Malik.
(*c*) See note 8. Azim Khan's elder brother Chaprai was one of the murdered Maliks.

* * * * * * * *

Bahlolzai, Aimal Khel, Nazar Khel, Aziz Khel, Fateh Khel

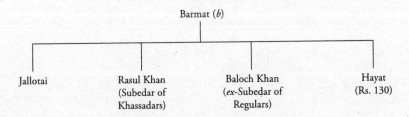

(*b*) In Mr Bruce's list of 1895 as a first class Malik.

Index